Mountains in the Mist

Books by Frank W. Boreham

The Luggage of Life
Mountains in the Mist
The Life Verses Series

Mountains in the Mist

F. W. BOREHAM

kregel
PUBLICATIONS

Grand Rapids, MI 49501

Mountains in the Mist by Frank W. Boreham.

Published in 1995 by Kregel Publications, a division of Kregel, Inc., P. O. Box 2607, Grand Rapids, MI 49501. Kregel Publications provides trusted, biblical publications for Christian growth and service. Your comments and suggestions are valued.

Cover Photo: Adam Jones Photography
Cover Design: Alan G. Hartman

Library of Congress Cataloging-in-Publication Data
Boreham, Frank W., 1871–1959.
    Mountains in the mist / F. W. Boreham.
        p.   cm.
    Originally published: New York: Abingdon Press, 19—?.
    1. Christian life. I. Title.
BV4501.B68544   1995   248.4—dc20   95-10490
                                                        CIP
    ISBN 0-8254-2163-2 (paperback)

1 2 3 4 5 Printing / Year 99 98 97 96 95

Printed in the United States of America

CONTENTS

By Way of Introduction 7

Part I

1. The Pageant Through the Bush 11
2. On Frightening Timothy 21
3. The Minor Minor Prophets 30
4. The Passing of the Impossible 38
5. Lead, Kindly Light 49
6. A Bush Philosopher 58
7. Spectre and Song 68
8. The Pioneer 75
9. The Exhilarations of Life 87

Part II

1. That Blessed Word—'Which?' 99
2. The Building of the Bridge 108
3. The Dainties in the Dungeon 120
4. Etiquette 131
5. Chrysanthemums 141
6. The Branch on the Breakers 151
7. The Baby 160
8. The Doctor 171
9. The Analyst 182
10. The Scavenger 191

6 **Contents**

Part III

1. Granny 203
2. 'Wullie!' 211
3. A Canary at the Pole 219
4. Hairbreadth Escapes 225
5. Escapes—*Not* Hairbreadth 236
6. Praying for Carlo 244
7. Mount Disappointment 254
8. Second-Class Passengers 265
9. The Poppies in the Corn 274

BY WAY OF INTRODUCTION

MANY a time, in nearing these Australian shores, or in cruising about the rugged and splintered coast of New Zealand, I have seen, as the first glimpse of land, the ghostly summits towering above filmy banks of cloud. The foreshore was hidden in the haze, and those spectral peaks were alone visible I have afterwards chatted with other men, who, never having seen those massive mountains, could nevertheless discourse quite learnedly about them. Geographers could tell me their names, their altitude, and the historical circumstances surrounding their discovery. Meteorologists explained to me their immense climatic importance. Botanists dilated upon the shrubs that draped their graceful slopes and upon the herbs that flourished in their thickly wooded valleys. Geologists unfolded the wondrous secrets of their strata. But, knowing nothing of this learned lore, it is something to have actually witnessed the wonder of the mountains and to have carried the impression of their grandeur in my heart for ever afterwards.

Other things too, I have seen, much as I saw
the mountains in the mist. With their precise
theological, philosophical, and scientific significance
I am not concerned. They have simply loomed up
grandly against the sky-line, and I have tried to set
down here the impressions that those hazy visions
have created.

FRANK W. BOREHAM.

Hobart Tasmania, 1914.

PART I

I

THE PAGEANT THROUGH THE BUSH

A THING happened the other evening that charmed and captivated me. I was journeying in the express on my way from Melbourne to Sydney. The train was gliding slowly past an up-country siding. Not a house was in sight. Far as the eye could see was nothing but the dense virgin bush, with just a rough track thridding its way among the giant trees. Suddenly I heard a tremendous shouting. Looking quickly out, I saw a little boy—a typical child of the bush—standing by the siding, with his hands to his mouth, yelling at the pitch of his voice: ' Paper! *Paper!* PAPER!' Some of the passengers, more accustomed to this kind of thing than I was, instantly flung up the windows, and threw out copies of the *Age* and of the *Argus*. And as I looked out of the carriage window I saw the little fellow—his face wreathed in satisfied smiles—gather up the papers, tuck them under his arm, and set off along the tortuous and dusty track among the trees towards the tiny settlement of which I could just see the smoke over the distant hills.

Now, this, as I have said, greatly interested me, and plunged me into a whirl of pleasant thought. Why did the people of that small settlement want the paper, and send the boy right down to the express to shout for it? Why could Bulman's Gully not be satisfied with Bulman's Gully? Why could Horseshoe Creek not be content with Horseshoe Creek? What do they want the *paper* for? The same phenomenon is nowhere to be seen beyond the limits of humanity. The sparrows of Australia show no spark of interest in their poorer kindred on the London house-tops. Our Tasmanian rabbits are coldly indifferent to the fate of their furry brethren on the mainland. The African lions never bother their heads about the tigers of Bengal. The brown kangaroos of our Australian wilds do not pine for tidings of the fallow deer on the upland lawns and in the forest glades of England. But with man it is quite otherwise. He must have his paper, and, even if he be buried in the deepest seclusion of the Never-Never Country, he will contrive some way of obtaining it. *He wants the world, and he won't be happy till he gets it.* The Australian squatter sits outside his lonely humpy, and hungers for Europe and Asia and America and

Africa, and for all the scattered islands of the rolling seas. He wants the Equator, and he wants the Poles. He craves for the Atlantic, and he thirsts for the Pacific. He must feel the throb of all your revolutions and tumults ; he must know of all your inventions and discoveries ; he must read of all your sports and politics ; he must peer into all your Courts and Cabinets ; he must follow all your travellers and explorers ; he must keep in touch with all your commerce and your industries ; he must see the list of your births and marriages and deaths. He hates to feel that any stick or stone or straw has really eluded him. He must have it all, *all*, ALL ; and he must have it all, *all* the time. It is a fearful and a wonderful thing—this insatiable craving of the human heart for the whole wide world. As I watched that little urchin from outback setting off along the dusty and rut-riddled track with his papers, each page crammed with cablegrams from everywhere, I saw all the nations on the face of the earth tramping in stately and imposing procession along that lonely path. It was one of the most gorgeous pageants that I have ever gazed upon. White men and black men, brown men and yellow men, pale men and swarthy men ; men of the prairie and men of the veldt ; men of the city and men of the woods : men from the deserts and men from the snows; men of all tribes and tongues, of all latitudes and languages, swept in their millions past the swaying blue-gums and vanished over the ridge! I beheld splendid empires, ancient dynasties, rising republics; all pouring their pulsing life, by means of these newspapers, into every little hut and homestead in that isolated settlement. It was grand! And more than this I saw. For it seemed to me that, just as a puddle may reflect a planet, I had mirrored in this rural idyll one of the most impressive and suggestive mysteries that the universe can hold.

The aching hunger of the human heart for the whole wide world! It is a positively fearsome thing. Many illustrations rush to memory, but the most clear and the most classical is that of David Livingstone. What a day that was when, after his long seclusion in the forests of Central Africa, he was at last found by Stanley! Let Stanley himself tell the great story:

'The doctor asked me to tell him the news. "No, doctor," said I, "read your home letters first; you must be impatient for them!"

'"Ah," said Livingstone, "I have waited for years for letters. I can wait a few hours longer. No, tell me general news: *how's the world getting on?*"'

And then, buried in that African jungle, the two
men sat for hours whilst the one told the other of the
completion of the great Pacific railroad, of Grant's
election to the Presidency, of the realization of
electric cables, of the Franco-German war, of the
siege of Paris, of the Cretan rebellion, of the sensational developments in Egypt, of the Spanish
revolution which had driven Isabella from the
throne, of the assassination of General Prim, and
of a hundred other historic transformations. Even
as Stanley told the story, Livingstone became a
changed man. Fresh tides of vitality rushed into
his frame ; his appetite strangely returned to him ;
his haggard face simply shone with the glow of
human enthusiasm. ' You have brought me new
life ! You have brought me new life ! You have
brought me new life ! ' he repeated again, and again,
and again. What did it all mean ? It meant this.
The heart of a man cries out for the world, the whole
wide world ; and it is starved if you confine it to
the African forest or the Australian bush. A geographical fragment will not appease its hunger. A
continent isn't enough. Stanley poured *the world*
into the empty soul of Livingstone ; and every fibre
and sinew of his being tingled with new animation
and fresh energy. It is a very wonderful thing—
this restlessness that we feel in the morning until

we have seen the newspaper, this hunger for the
world, of which every tiny hamlet and each bush
settlement is so deeply and intensely conscious.

Now, what is it, this deep and terrible craving of
ours ? And whence came it ? There is but one
answer possible. Man is made in the image of
God And this human hunger for the world is
the image and echo and reflection of the *divine*
hunger for the world. The child in a squalid London
slum puts the shell to his ear, and his eyes sparkle
as he listens to the roar and murmur of distant
oceans. Uncrossed seas and unplumbed depths
stir his imprisoned fancy. I turn my eyes in upon
my own soul when I catch myself longing for the
newspaper ; and in that yearning for the world I
catch a faint pulsation of the hunger of the Infinite.
There is one noble and mountainous scripture that
always looms largely on the horizon of inspiration.
It stands boldly out from all its companions, as
Mount Everest towers above the Himalayas. It
is this, ' God so loved *the World* . . .' Is that not
a wonderfully wonderful word ? It takes God to
love the world. An Englishman may love his dear
old Mother-Country ; a German may love his
Fatherland ; but who can love *the World* ? Why,
there are scores of tribes and peoples on the face
of the earth whose very names would surprise

us if we heard them. How can we love them? But God loves them because He knows them. We always love people if we know them. It is always safe to conclude, if we do not love a man, that it is because we do not know him. I like to think, as I walk down the crowded street, that every soul I meet, however commonplace or unattractive, is all the world to somebody. Somebody loves him because somebody knows him. And, to that somebody, heaven would be no heaven without him. The world is a very lovable place, and its people are very lovable people. We do not know the world, and therefore we do not love the world. But 'God so knows the world' and therefore 'God so loved the world . . .' I love God the more because He loves the world I live in; and I love the world the more because it is transfigured by the love of God.

There is no world, among all the worlds, to be compared with this world. I am sure of that. The most pressing and unanimous call to Jupiter or Venus or Mars or Saturn will not tempt me to go if I can, by any frantic argument or artifice or manœuvre, induce my fellow mortals to allow me to remain here a little longer. This is *the* world; there can be no possible doubt about that. 'God so loved *the* world '—that is to say, He loved *this one*.

That is lovely ! I revel in that thought. God has
sprinkled the world with beautiful and gracious
women ; but, whilst He has given each of us men
the power to admire them all, we are each of us able
to love only one of them supremely. May not this
also be a reflection, an echo, an indication that we
are fashioned after the image and similitude of the
Most High ? For God has sprinkled His universe
with beautiful worlds, as He has sprinkled this
world with beautiful women. There are millions
upon millions of them. And when God gazed upon
the galaxies of worlds that He had made, He saw that
they were very good. He looked admiringly upon
worldhood, as we men gaze admiringly upon womanhood. And then with one of His worlds He fell in
love. He loved it supremely, loved it with a love
so fond, and so awful, and so deep, and so eternal,
that we catch our breath as we think of it ! He
loved it with a love that led to the inexpressible
mystery of Bethlehem, to the unutterable anguish
of Gethsemane, to the unspeakable tragedy of
Calvary. ' God so loved the world that He gave
His only begotten Son.' In the light of that stupendous declaration the world seems a terrible
place. It seems a solemn and a sacred thing to be
living in that one world towards which God Himself
felt so tenderly ! The place whereon we stand is

holy ground ! And yet, after all, it is not the place. It is the people. It is ourselves. It is you. It is I. That is the rapture of it. ' He loved *me*, and gave Himself for *me* ! ' As Faber sings :

> All this God is all for me,
> A Saviour all my own.

True love is always the uttermost simplicity to the lover, and it is always the profoundest mystery to the loved. ' God so loved the world.' ' He loved me.' It may be all as plain as plain can be to *Him* ; but to the world, to us—to you, to me—there must always abide a concentrated infinity of mystery in such amazing words as these.

I am just beginning to understand this longing of mine for the latest intelligence, this hunger that I feel for the world. I begin to comprehend the instinct that prompted that wayside cry for the newspapers. There is something sublime, something divine about it. The movement of a great steamer on the open sea causes a commotion on the waters that sends the wash of a wave to a distant shore. This cry of the heart for all the continents and islands is but the wash of the wave. And when I lift up my eyes to see what causes the foaming commotion by the surge, I see this stupendous fact, ' *God so loved the world* . . .' If this tremendous verity does not inspire and inflame our enthusiasm for the conquest of the world, nothing will.   In a sweet and graceful Eastern story we are told how Abraham's servant gazed with wistful eyes upon the beauty of Rebekah, and longed to win her for Isaac, his young lord.   When the Church comes to understand the love with which God loved the world. she will be restless and ill at ease until all the great empires have been captured, until every coral island has been won.

II

ON FRIGHTENING TIMOTHY

IT is an evil thing and a bitter to frighten Timothy.
And it is wofully easy to do it. Timothy is very
young. He always was! He always will be!
Timothy has solved the problem of perpetual
youth. He will never grow old. He was very
young when he went up to Corinth that first time.
Paul felt sorry for him. He was such a boy. '*If
Timothy come,*' the wise old man wrote to those
Corinthian Christians, anticipating their amazement
as they beheld the boyish ambassador, '*if Timothy
come, see that he be with you without fear. Let no
man despise him.*' And ten years later poor Timothy
is still in trouble about his perennial juvenility.
' Let no man despise thy youth,' Paul writes again
in this later letter. It is very beautiful. The
boyishness of Timothy is chronic, inveterate, incur-
able. He simply won't grow old. He was very
young when Paul sent him to Corinth. He was
still blushing over his boyish bearing when the

veteran addressed to him his last pathetic letter.
And he was still young when I myself met him. And
just because there are still so many Corinthians
who despise poor Timothy's youth, it is still necessary for Paul to beg and entreat those thoughtless
believers not to frighten Timothy. ' *If Timothy
come, see that he be with you without fear.*'

' *If Timothy come,*' says Paul. And Timothy
often comes. I met him once as a young convert,
setting himself with great hesitation, and with much
trembling, to the high and holy enterprise of local
preaching. I met him again as a young home
missionary, encountering insuperable obstacles in
his large and lonely district in the Never-Never
Country, yet not half as much afraid of the muddy
roads and impassable fords as of the peril of un-
faithfulness among his scattered people. I met
him again as a student pastor, burdening himself,
after the heavy scholastic toils of the week, with
the spiritual oversight of a pastorless congregation
on the Lord's Day. And I met him once as a
young minister, fresh from college, pulling himself
together after the solemn and searching ordeal of
his induction, and wondering who, among saints or
angels, was sufficient for these dreadful things. Poor
Timothy ! Paul felt very sorry for him. So did I.

' *If Timothy come, see that he be with you without*

fear.' Timothy is very shy, very sensitive, very
timid. At least, so all the commentators say, and
if they don't know, who should? Yes, I feel sure
that they are right. It is impossible to read of
Paul's tender solicitude for Timothy without being
driven to that conclusion. Timothy is very shy, and
very sensitive, and very timid. All the most winsome and most lovable things are. The birds on the
bough, the rabbits in their burrow, the deer in the
forest glades—all the feathered and furry creatures
to which we feel irresistibly and instinctively drawn
—are shy, and timid, and shrinking. And so is
Timothy. ' *If Timothy come, see that he be with you
without fear.'*

Some day, when I have a Sunday to spare, I mean
to run down to that bush congregation, to that
country pastorate, to that suburban out-station, at
which Timothy usually preaches. I should like to
have a quiet talk with the people about this matter
of frightening Timothy. I cannot persuade myself
that they fully recognize the gracious opportunity
which Timothy's presence offers to them. It may
be theirs to foster, and cherish, and nurture in him
all that is most spiritual, and tender, and noble, and
Christlike ; and to send him forth at last from their
tearful farewell meeting, not only with a silver-
mounted umbrella or a Gladstone bag, but with a

spirit sweetened, and instructed, and enriched in preparation for a great and fruitful ministry. Nor do I feel quite sure that they recognize the weight of their responsibility. They may quite easily and innocently spoil Timothy. They may frighten him out of all that is best in him. And they may dispatch him at last from their farewell meeting with a very beautiful silver-mounted umbrella, or a very handsome Gladstone bag—*and with nothing else.* And neither a silver-mounted umbrella nor a Gladstone bag is a quite adequate preparation for the Christian ministry in strenuous days like these.

It is a dreadful thing to frighten Timothy out of his dreams, his ambitions, his ideals. He always has them. There is nothing else to attract him into the ministry. It is perfectly safe to assume that when Timothy boards the train that will bear him to his country pastorate, his head is full of the most beautiful ideas as to what a Christian minister should be. He has been reading Richard Baxter, or William Law, or Alexander Whyte, or the Yale Lectures. Or at least he has been reading his Bible, and he feels it a fearful thing to be called to follow in the footsteps of the Old Testament prophets and the New Testament preachers. And he has prayed until his face has shone that he may show himself worthy of so solemn and sacred a charge. And all

this thinking and dreaming and talking and reading and praying have but enlarged his heart, and
inflamed his emotions, and heightened his ambitions.
And with all this wealth of spiritual fervour surging,
like a tumult of flood-water, through every fibre of
his being, he sets his face towards his mission district or student pastorate. And when Paul sees
him setting out in this temper, he trembles for him.
Such a spirit is very fragile. It would be so easy
for those thoughtless but well-meaning people at
Corinth to frighten it all out of him. ' *If Timothy
come, see that he be with you without fear.*'

In his amazingly candid autobiography Benjamin
Franklin tells an ugly story. He has been describing
his passionate and methodical struggle after goodness.
And then he likens himself to ' my neighbour who,
in buying an axe of a smith, desired to have the whole
of its surface as bright as the edge. The smith
consented to grind it bright for him, if he would turn
the wheel. He turned, while the smith pressed the
broad face of the axe hard and heavily on the stone,
which made the turning of it very fatiguing. The
man came every now and then from the wheel to
see how the work went on. At length, he said he
would take his axe as it was, without further grinding. " No," said the smith, " turn on, turn on, we
shall **have** it bright by and by ; as yet it is only

speckled." "Yes," said the exhausted man, "but
I think, after all, *I like a speckled axe best!*"
Now, I have heard that there have been such tragedies as *failures* in the Christian ministry—men
who have lost the rapture, and the vision, and the
glory. Such things might move an angel's tears.
But I wonder in how many of these cases Timothy
was frightened. The conversation at Corinth was
so exclusively about finance and trivialities and
externals, and he met with so little real comrade-
ship and spiritual response, that he unconsciously
adjusted his standard to fit his environment, and
determined to content himself with a speckled axe.

I fancy that the most intense peril lurks in the
matter of pastoral visitation. Timothy has come
to think of such a visit as a very beautiful affair.
He imagines that he will be straightway taken into
the inmost confidences of the home. His advice
may be asked ; at any rate, his sympathies will be
invited. He pictures himself reading an appropriate
scripture, pointing out, it may be, in a sentence or
two, its wealthy encouragement to the dwellers
in this particular homestead. And then, surrounded
by parents and children, he sees himself bowing in
prayer, and pouring out his soul in earnest inter-
cession on behalf of the family clustered around him.
This is Timothy's dream. And it will be a tragedy

of the worst kind if the people of Corinth frighten
him out of it.   If they are awake to recognize the day
of their visitation, they will put themselves to some
trouble to make Timothy's dream come true as soon
as he knocks at the door.   It will be a fine thing for
him, and a fine thing for them.   But——.   But
let me venture on a parable.   In the depths of a
Brazilian forest stood a giant tree.   Its branches
were ablaze with the most glorious orchids.   They
grew out of every crack and crevice in the old
tree's bark.   It was a riot of radiant colour.   One
morning the sun rose upon it, glorifying its dazzling
charms.   Birds of every note filled its branches,
and flooded the valley with liquid song.   Other birds
of brilliant plumage passed to and fro among the
sunlit branches, like flashes of golden flame.   It
was a picture of Paradise.   Then arose a sound of
swishing boughs and crackling twigs.   The gaiety
was hushed on the instant.   A troop of apes invaded
the sylvan solitude.   The birds flew in terror.   The
gorgeous petals were soon scattered in all directions.
The glade re-echoed with the meaningless jabbering
of the monkeys.   The song was dead, and the forest
seemed very poor.   I fancy I have seen something
like that happen, although I have never been to
Brazil.   It is easy to frighten the poetry out of the
soul of Timothy.   It is easy to quench his fires.   It

is a pitiful thing when chatter takes the place of
song.

Ian Maclaren has a lovely story of John Carmichael
that I somehow think would have been very much
to Paul's taste as he thought of Timothy and his
peril at Corinth. Now, Carmichael was like Timothy,
very young, very shy, very sensitive, and very
shrinking. He entered upon his first charge. But
he felt—painfully, acutely, constantly—the awful
chasm that yawned between his radiant dreams and
his actual achievements. And he felt that the
people must be regarding him either with pity or
contempt. One Sabbath, as he was sitting in the
vestry, all the elders filed solemnly in. He felt that
they had come to tell him that they could tolerate
it no longer. Then the sagest and kindliest of them
all addressed him. They had noticed his fearful-
ness, and nervousness, and timidity, and wished
him to be completely at his ease. Was he not among
his own people ? They would have Timothy among
them without fear. ' You are never to be troubled
in the pulpit,' the old man went on, ' or be thinking
about anything but the word of the Lord and
the souls of the people, of which you are the shep-
herd. We will ask you to remember, when you
stand in your place to speak to us in the name of
the Lord, that as the smoke goeth up from the

homes of the people in the morning, so will their prayers be ascending for their minister, and as you look down upon us before you begin to speak, maybe you will say to yourself, next Sabbath, "They are all loving me." Oh, yes, and it will be true from the oldest to the youngest, *we will all be loving you very much.*' 'And *that*,' Ian Maclaren says, '*that* is why John Carmichael remained in the ministry of Jesus Christ, the most patient and mindful of ministers.' And I, for one, can easily believe it.

III

THE MINOR MINOR PROPHETS

IT was the deliberate opinion of Charley Bates, the pickpocket, that Bill Sikes' dog was ' *an out-and-out Christian*.'

' He wouldn't so much as bark in a witness-box for fear of committing himself ; no, not if you tied him up in one, and left him there without wittles for a fortnight,' added the Artful Dodger.

' He's an out-and-out Christian,' said Charley.

I do not quite understand why I have begun this chapter with Bill Sikes' dog. I meant to have written about Balaam's ass. I must apologize to my readers for having introduced the wrong animal. But now that we have Bill Sikes' dog here, we may as well have a good look at him. For there is a distinct connexion between the two after all ; and, personally, I always find it more easy to understand the record of the wayward prophet and his eloquent beast when I think of it with the story of Bill Sikes and his dog open before me.

' Yes, he's an out-and-out Christian ! ' said Charley.

I am inclined to go one step farther than did Charley. I propose to establish a new order, to be called *The Minor Minor Prophets*. And among those Minor Minor Prophets both Balaam's ass and Sikes' dog will find honourable places.

Principal George Adam Smith, of Aberdeen—our greatest living authority on Hebrew prophecy—says that the two indispensable qualifications of a prophet are Vision and Voice. Your prophet *sees* what others cannot *see*, and therefore he *says* what others cannot *say*. Now, those are precisely the features about these Minor Minor Prophets that impress me most. Their vision is positively uncanny, and they say things unutterable. Balaam's ass is by no means alone in that respect.

I do not keep a dog. It is too humiliating. A man cannot possibly enjoy the companionship of a dog and maintain his self-respect. Walk along a country road with a dog, and he will discover, and draw your attention to, a hundred things to which you were totally blind. Every broken stick, every mark in the mud, every scratch in the sand, every gap in the hedge, every fluttering leaf, means something to the dog. It is his way of reading history. He knows exactly what has happened, and what is happening now, and what is going to happen A wonderful seer is he. It is positively painful.

He makes his owner feel like a dolt and a dullard.
It is the story of Balaam over again. The ass saw
the angel, but Balaam didn't. Any man who keeps
a dog, or a horse, or a minor minor prophet of any
kind knows that this sort of thing happens very
often.

Travellers tell us that a horse or a donkey is never
deceived by a mirage. And just because these Minor
Minor Prophets see so much more than we can see,
they say so much more than we can say   I have
never been able to sympathize with those who
find a difficulty in the eloquence of Balaam's ass.
When I was a child I pored over Aesop's fables, and it
seemed the most natural thing in the world to me
that the wolves and the foxes, the dogs and the
horses, the storks and the cranes, should speak
to each other and to men. I do not remember ever
pausing to think about it : it seemed so perfectly
and exquisitely fitting and right. Then followed
that silly and superior stage in which we doubt
everything that we had ever believed. And during
that period I, of course, turned up my nose con-
temptuously at my childish simplicity, and assured
myself that it was all nonsense. How could animals
speak ? The idea was preposterous. Then came
wisdom, or, at least, an inkling of it. I remembered
that the history of the world was crammed with

just such stories as the story of Balaam's ass. Did
not geese call up the slumbering Roman guards and
save the capitol ?   Did not a spaniel cry aloud and
spare not—after the fashion of a major prophet—
until he had saved a nation from disgrace ?   The
Prince of Orange and all his sentries slept.   The
Spanish soldiers were within striking distance.
And in that moment of imminent peril, on which
the destinies of nations trembled, the Prince's spaniel
spake out bravely.   ' To his dying day,' says
Motley, ' the Prince ever afterwards kept a spaniel
of the same race in his bed-chamber.'   I came, too,
upon Luther's tribute to his robin.   ' I have one
preacher,' he says, ' that I love better than any other
upon earth ; it is my little tame robin, which
preaches to me daily.   I put his crumbs upon my
window-sill, especially at night.   He hops on to
the sill when he wants his supply, and takes as much
as he desires to satisfy his need.   From thence
he always hops on to a little tree close by, and lifts
up his voice to God and sings his carol of praise and
gratitude, tucks his little head under his wing, and
goes fast to sleep, and leaves to-morrow to look after
itself.   He is the best preacher that I have on earth.'
And then, my scepticism almost gone, and my mind
swinging rapidly back to my childhood's faith, I
came upon Bill Sikes' dog.   How reproachfully he

used to look up into the burglar's face ! Tell me
that these Minor Minor Prophets cannot speak !
Call them ' dumb creatures ' ! I have heard a dog
say more in two seconds than I could express in two
minutes or write in two pages ! Does not a pointer
say more than a parrot ? To be sure ! These
creatures are no more dumb than Balaam's ass.
Like him, they are Minor Minor Prophets. They
have Vision and they have Voice. If we think them
dumb, it is because we ourselves are *deaf* ; that is all.

Yes, they have Voice. And no man who has heard
these Minor Minor Prophets can afford to ignore their
message. Let me give one startling and tremendous
illustration. I sometimes think it the most sensational thing in literature. A hundred years ago
there took place Napoleon's historic and memorable
retreat from Moscow. Among those frozen mountain passes, and along those deep and shadowy
valleys in which the drifted snow had buried the
very pine-trees, Napoleon strewed the corpses of
half a million men. It is the most stupendous
tragedy that the history of the world can produce.
Did no prophet rise up in those days to warn the
Emperor that his invasion of Russia would be attended by so enormous and appalling a catastrophe ?
There *were* prophets to warn him ! God never lets
any man, much less half a million men, rush to his

dreadful doom without sending some prophet to
warn and deliver him. He sent Minor Minor Prophets.   Listen !   Frank Buckland, the great
naturalist, who knew the Minor Minor Prophets
thoroughly, says : ' If the Emperor Napoleon, when
on the road to Moscow, had condescended to observe
the flights of storks and cranes passing over his fated
battalions, subsequent events in the politics of
Europe might have been very different. These
storks and cranes knew of the coming on of a great
and terrible winter ; the birds hastened towards
the south, but Napoleon and his huge army pressed
on northwards.' And we Australians remember
gratefully the pigeon that, up in the dusty heart of
the continent, showed Captain Sturt where the
water was, and saved the life of the greatest of all
our explorers.   We gladly welcome that gentle bird,
with its keen vision and its soft voice, to the goodly
fellowship of the Minor Minor Prophets.
    Balaam thrashed the ass, and Bill Sikes kicked
the dog.   That is always the fate of the prophets,
even of the Minor Minor Prophets.   Indeed, it was
not owing to the virtue of either Balaam or Bill
Sikes that the ass and the dog—poor Minor Minor
Prophets—did not fare even worse.   ' Balaam said
unto the ass : I would there were a sword in mine
hand, for now would I kill thee ! '   And Bill Sikes

did actually prepare to drown the dog; had the
stone and the string and the water all ready;
but the dog—having a prophetic gift on which the
burglar had not reckoned—mysteriously vanished.
We are born persecutors. It comes quite naturally
to us to stone the prophets. It is very absurd.
We might just as well smash the mirror if it dares
to suggest that we are not as handsome as Apollo
or as beautiful as Venus! But absurd and illogical
as it all is, we do it. We are like Macaulay's Hindu
who, seeing the sacred water of the Ganges under a
microscope, smashed the microscope! And so poor
Balaam thrashed his ass, and longed to slay him!
And so poor Bill Sikes kicked his dog, and tried to
drown him! And so—and on precisely identical
principles—all your persecutions have been inau-
gurated. Those roaring lions at Rome, that hideous
inquisition in Spain, those blazing fires at Smith-
field—it is the same sad and silly old story, over and
over and over again.

There was a Prophet once, the peerless Prince of all
the prophets. And all the prophets of all the ages
reverently salute Him. He possessed the two great
essentials. He had Vision such as no prophet,
before or since, ever enjoyed. And Voice; for it was
like the sound of many waters. Beneath the magic
of His utterance wicked men winced and weeping

women were wondrously comforted. But they crucified Him! His path led to the Cross. It reached its climax on Calvary. That is always the way. The *Prince* of the prophets, and the *major* prophets, and the *minor* prophets, and even the *minor minor* prophets, must all pay that same dread penalty for Truth's dear sake. And I for my part am face to face with a terrible choice. Shall I take my stand with those noble souls—prophets and heroes and martyrs—who have seen clearly and spoken truly, come what may? Or shall I be found skulking among those who wince beneath the word, slash savagely at the faithful speaker, and stagger blindly out into the dark?

' He's an out-and-out Christian ! ' said Charley Bates, the pickpocket, as he discussed Bill Sikes' dog with his friend, the Artful Dodger. His bald and dogmatic affirmation may be open to theological criticism ; but I am in no mood at this moment to take up the cudgels against him.

IV

THE PASSING OF THE IMPOSSIBLE

LONG, long ago, when simple and primitive peoples found room in their folk-lore for hobgoblins, unicorns, witches, and trolls, there were those who were actually sufficiently superstitious to believe that such things as ' *impossibilities* ' really existed. These milestones in the progress of the race from barbarism to civilization are most fascinating ! Of course *we* know, being the Christians that we are, that there is no such thing as an impossibility in the world or out of it. An impossibility is an impossibility. Impossibilities belong to the realm of mythology. They inhabit the same weird world as the brownies and the elves, the fairies and the ghouls. As serious and scientific and practical and believing men, we must frankly confess to ourselves that the very notion of an impossibility is, on the face of it, a ludicrous absurdity. I know that Professor Dryasdust will hotly challenge my conclusion. He will crush me, to his own entire satisfaction, by saying that a triangle with four sides

is an impossibility. But poor old Professor Dryasdust really does not know what he is talking about !
He most certainly does not know what he is talking
about when he talks of a triangle with four sides.
For a triangle with four sides is a contradiction in
terms, a mere mental aberration, a confusion of
incomprehensible sounds, a mathematical gibberish,
an intellectual Borrioboola-Gha. There is no such
thing as a triangle with four sides. There is no such
thing as an impossibility. Professor Dryasdust is
right after all. The triangle with four sides and the
impossibility stand or fall together. They fall.

Nothing is impossible. The very word is relative
and not absolute. It was simply impossible yesterday to do the things that we do with ease to-day.
And the very fact that we do them with ease to-day
proves that they were not really impossible yesterday. We cannot do to-day what our children will
do to-morrow. But the fact that our children will
do those things to-morrow shows that they are not
absolutely, but merely relatively, impossible to-day.
Leander would have considered it impossible to
have crossed the Hellespont in an aeroplane !
But it wasn't ! He didn't know how to do it,
that was all ! Julius Caesar would have regarded
it as impossible to flash his famous ' Veni, vidi, vici '
to the Senate by wireless ! But it wasn't ! The

only trouble was that he didn't know how ! Homer would have supposed that it was impossible to write the *Iliad* with a fountain pen, or to click off the *Odyssey* with a typewriter ! Nero never dreamed of driving down the Appian Way in a motor-car ! But these things were not impossibilities. *We* have demonstrated that. And our children's children will prove in like manner that the things that seem to us grotesquely impossible are as simple as simple can be. We may hope to become in time like Alice in Wonderland when she was pursuing the White Rabbit. ' For you see, so many out-of-the-way things had happened to her that Alice had begun to think that very few things indeed were really impossible.' It would do us all a world of good to chase white rabbits if, in doing so, we could all make the same splendid and invaluable discovery. Things are never impossible. The only obstacle is our own pitiful ignorance, or our own pitiful indolence.

' *It is utterly impossible !* ' said the natives of Central Africa to David Livingstone when the intrepid explorer proposed to cross the Kalahari Desert in the course of his first missionary journey. ' It is utterly impossible, even to us black men ! ' Livingstone smiled. He knew that impossibilities belong to the same realm as witches and trolls. He gathered around him his wife and little children, and, in their company, crossed that impossible desert !

' *It is utterly impossible !* ' said the Spanish priests to Columbus. ' We can prove from the Bible that a new hemisphere in the West is an absolute impossibility ! ' Yet there it was ; and Columbus found it !

' *It is utterly impossible !* ' said Augustine. ' I can prove from the inspired Scriptures that an antipodean world is an utter impossibility ! ' Yet here am I writing these words in Australia !

' *It is utterly impossible !* ' said some very learned doctors of the Church when a nest of consecrated cobblers suggested missions to the heathen. ' Savages can never be anything but savages ! ' To which let Henry Drummond's great chapter on ' The Dawn of Mind ' make answer. He instances people after people that have been suddenly transformed from abysmal depths of barbarism to high levels of civilization. ' The situation is dramatic ! ' he exclaims.

The fact is that the next step in human progress is always an invasion of the territory of the impossible. Always ! The directors of a shipping company, for example, propose to build a new vessel. The most brilliant and daring nautical architects in the world are summoned to their council-table. A plan is at length submitted. The directors, eager for the best, turn upon the architects. ' Is it not possible, gentlemen, to improve upon this in some particular ? ' ' It is absolutely impossible ! ' the architects reply. Yet, before the steamer is launched, proposals for the erection of a much more stately ship have been submitted ; and, by the time that the second vessel is ready for the sea, the first is ridiculed as old-fashioned and obsolete ! What has happened ? We have invaded the impossible, that is all. To send a telegram would have seemed a screaming impossibility to our great-grandfathers. To send a telegram without wires would have seemed just as quixotic to their sons. But, one after the other, each frontier was happily crossed. Yes ; the next step in the progress of the world is always an invasion of the impossible. When Lord Russell of Killowen and Sir Frank Lockwood visited Mr. Edison, he told them that he never attempted possible things. Impossibilities were the only things worth trying ! Mr. Edgar A. Guest has finely sung :

> Somebody said that it couldn't be done,
>   But he with a chuckle replied,
> That ' maybe it couldn't, but he would be one
>   Who wouldn't say so till he tried.'

So he buckled right in with the trace of a grin
   On his face. If he worried he hid it.
He started to sing as he tackled the thing
   That couldn't be done—and he did it !

Why, when you come to think of it, we are for
ever and ever doing impossibilities. We are at it
morning, noon, and night. It is one of our most inveterate habits. The food we eat, the clothes we
wear, the papers we read, the engines we drive, the
houses in which we live, and the conveyances in
which we ride—all have emerged from the embryonic
condition of impossibilities. Yet here they all are !
If any reader is inclined to suspect that a real live
impossibility does somewhere lurk among the
shadows of the solar system, let him begin his
education all over again. Let him reach from its
obscure shelf a book that enchained his fancy in his
infancy. I mean the *Water Babies*. That second
chapter is a capital piece of writing. And it abounds
with illustrations that are right into our hands at
this point. 'The truth is,' Kingsley concludes,
' that we fancy that such and such things cannot be
simply because we have not seen them, just as a
savage fancies that there cannot be such a thing as a
locomotive because he never saw one running wild
in the forest.'

Now, there is one text among the great sayings

of Jesus that I confess I never understood until very
lately : ' Verily, I say unto you, if ye have faith
as a grain of mustard-seed, ye shall say unto this
mountain, Remove hence to yonder place ; and it
shall remove ; and nothing shall be impossible unto
you.' Now, I was so incredulous about the possibility of removing mountains that I had to see it
done before I really and truly believed. I am
writing in Tasmania. And here in Tasmania we
have a mountain—Mount Lyell. And gradually a
strange faith stole into the hearts of men. They
believed that underneath Mount Lyell there was an
abundance of copper. They suspected it. They
investigated it. They *believed* it ! And when they
really *believed* it, they actually said unto the mountain, ' Remove hence into yonder place ! ' They
believed ; they moved the mountain ; and nothing
was impossible to them. The men who drove the
spectral impossibilities from the shadows of our
civilization were great believers, all of them. Columbus did not believe in the new world because he discovered it ; he discovered it because he first of all
believed it. Sir James Simpson believed that it was
possible to perform the ghastliest operations pain-
lessly. And he invented chloroform. Marconi,
Röntgen, Edison, and the rest all believed that
certain things were possible. And they soon

actualized their creeds. Their mirages became pools. All human experience goes to show that ' nothing is impossible to him that believeth.'

Now, all this proves that we are living in a very possible world. Its people are possible people ; its problems are possible problems ; its tasks are possible tasks. Yes, its tasks are possible tasks, even the greatest of them. Nothing has militated against the Christian conquest of the world more powerfully than the secret suspicion that the splendid enterprise is impossible. That dark nightmare always paralyses. Great achievers were ever great believers. And great believers were ever prodigious workers. Let them but believe, though it be only in copper, and they will move mountains.

The history of missions is one continuous story of the invasion of the impossible. Take three illustrations : (1) When Robert Moffat set out for Namaqualand, the people of the Cape wept over his certain destruction. 'The great chief Africaner will tear you to pieces ! ' they cried. ' He will strip off your skin and make a drum of it to dance to ! ' said one. ' He will make a drinking-cup of your skull ! ' exclaimed another. Yet in a few weeks Moffat and Africaner were partners in the sweetest Christian fellowship, and comrades in devoted

Christian service !   (2) And again, there is no ghastlier page in our missionary annals than the story of Liwanika and the Barotse people.   Read Coillard's letters to Arnot.   I once heard Arnot tell the story.   ' I do not know what is in store for these poor tribes,' Coillard writes.   ' The horizon is dark, and the sky very stormy ;   it seems as if we were witnessing the last days of the Barotse nation. . . . Liwanika has exterminated his enemies, even those whom he feared might one day become his enemies. I never saw such bloodthirsty people.'   It is a grim and ugly story of ceaseless brutality, cruelty, and carnage.   Yet a few years later that very chief, Liwanika, as a Christian ruler, represented his people, as a Christian people, at the Coronation of King Edward in Westminster Abbey, and went out of his way to show practical sympathy with all aggressive missionary enterprises.   (3) Henry Martyn once said that he would as soon expect to see one rise from the dead as to see a Brahmin become a Christian.   Yet in the very pagoda where a century ago Henry Martyn kneeled in prayer, Christian Brahmins from every province in India recently met to organize a native missionary society under native management, and to be supported entirely by native money !   Who believes in impossibilities after that ?

Is the immediate conquest of the world possible ?
The question is ridiculous. The world contains
millions of Christians. But the task does not need
millions. Millions ought to be able to evangelize the
entire universe. Fifty men of the stamp of Paul and
Xavier and Wesley would make Christ known to
every living soul on the face of the earth in twenty
years. That is our shame. If I could call spirits
from the vasty deep, and if they would come when
I did call for them, I would undertake to summon to
the task a hundred heroes who would make the whole
wide world ring with the praise of Christ, whilst we
were still droning over our minute-books. It is the
indisputable possibility of the task that makes
our tragic failure so shockingly humiliating. Yes,
it is all quite clear. We simply need to visit the
Delectable Mountains with Christiana and her
party, and to climb Mount Marvel, ' where was a
man who tumbled the hills about to show pilgrims
how to tumble their difficulties out of their way.'
This redoubtable son of Great Grace knew perfectly
well that there is no room in the universe—nor in a
million universes—for both a God and an impossibility. If you are quite sure of God, there is no
crack or crevice among all His worlds that can
harbour an impossibility. Atheism alone is the
religion of the impossible ; and, for that very

reason, it is an impossible religion. No man yet born has a faith roomy enough to permit of his believing in God and in the impossible at one and the same time. All things are possible to him that believeth.

V

LEAD, KINDLY LIGHT

At two most crucial points Christianity fearlessly
challenges experiment, and bravely dares a test.
The first is in the matter of *Prayer*. The second is
in the matter of *Guidance*. If it can be proved that
the great Father ever allows any of His children to
cry to Him in vain, or if it can be shown that He
leaves any of them to stumble home in the dark as
best they can, then Christianity has broken down.
It stands exposed and exploded. But can it?
There is no cause for alarm. In *The Luggage of Life*
I have tried to show that even in our dear earthly
homes, however crowded with cots they may become,
each child finds a place of his own, and his voice is
loved and listened to. The largeness of the family
does not diminish the affection for the individual ;
and earthly parentage is, after all, but a spark from
the divine flame. It is inconceivable that the Father
of fatherhood will overlook one of His children
simply because He has ' so much to see to.' It is our
Lord's own tender and beautiful argument : ' If ye

then, being evil . . . *how much more* shall your
heavenly Father ? ' Could anything be more satis-
fying or convincing ?

But to come to the second matter. We have
all known the torture of indecision. To buy or
not to buy ? To accept or to decline ? To go or to
stay ? To turn this way or that ? It is dreadful !
Now, the question is : Are we justified, in our sea-
sons of perplexity, in expecting to hear a guiding
voice, or to discern a shining light, or to see a beckoning hand ? Must we plunge into the gloom, or may
we follow the gleam ? Is there a Kindly Light that
leads ? If we reply in the negative, a hundred
exceeding great and precious promises become instantly unintelligible, and, in consequence, all
Scripture falls under suspicion of being disingenuous
and insincere. And yet, on the other hand, it
is so difficult, in our distraction, to hear that voice,
to discern that light, to see that beckoning hand.
Think of that memorable day in the life of Goethe.
' A delicious sadness subdued his thoughts,' his
biographer tells us, ' as he wandered dreamily along
the banks of the Lahn. The lovely scenes which
met his eye solicited his pencil, awakening once more
the ineffectual desire, which from time to time
aunted him, of becoming a painter. The desire,
often suppressed, now rose up in such serious shape

that he resolved to settle for ever whether he should devote himself to art or not. The test was curious. The river glided beneath, now flashing in the sunlight, now partially concealed by willows. Taking a knife from his pocket, he flung it with his left hand into the river, having previously resolved that, if he saw it fall, he was to become an artist ; but if the sinking knife was concealed by the willows, he was to abandon the idea. No ancient oracle was ever more ambiguous than the answer now given him. The willows concealed the sinking knife ; but the water splashed up like a fountain, and was distinctly visible. So indefinite an answer left him still in doubt.' It is thus that our wayward will-o'-the-wisps torment us. There must be a more excellent way. There is ! I hazard three suggestions.

I

The Kindly Light must be treated *very patiently*. May I draw upon my memory ? Just after I settled in my New Zealand manse it was my great privilege to entertain one of the most gifted, most experienced, and most gracious of our ministers. I felt it to be a priceless opportunity, and I sought his counsel concerning all my early ministerial difficulties. One lovely morning we were sitting together on the verandah, looking away across the golden plains to the purple and sunlit mountains, when I broached to him this very question. ' Can a man be quite sure,' I asked, ' that, in the hour of perplexity, he will be *rightly led* ?   Can he feel secure against *a false step* ? '   I shall never forget his reply. He sprang from his deck chair and came earnestly towards me. ' I am certain of it,' he exclaimed, ' if he will but *give God time* ! Remember *that* as long as you live,' he added entreatingly—' GIVE GOD TIME ! '

More than ten years later I found myself face to face with a crisis.   I had to make a decision on which my whole life's work depended, and I had to make the decision by five o'clock—the hour at which the telegraph office closed—on a certain Saturday evening. It chanced once more that a minister was my guest. But he could not help me. He thought it vastly improbable that God could concern Himself about individual trivialities. ' The Lord has so much to see to . . . such a lot of beds in the ward ! ' He was inclined to think that a certain element of chance dominated our mortality, that a man was bound to take certain risks, and that life was very much like a lottery. ' And if a man make a mistake at a critical juncture like this ? ' I asked anxiously. He shrugged his shoulders.

' And after that the dark.' I remember with a
shudder how my faith winced and staggered under
that blow. But I thought of the sunny morning
on the verandah ten years before, and clutched
desperately and wildly at my old faith. Saturday
came. I positively had not the ghost of a notion
as to what I ought to do. At five minutes to five
I was at the telegraph office, still in hopeless confusion. At three minutes to five a man rode up on a
bicycle. So far as I knew, he was absolutely igno-
rant of the crisis through which I was floundering.
But he told me something that relieved the entire
situation, and made my course as clear as noonday,
and by five o'clock the message had been dispatched.

Dr. Jowett, of New York, says that he was once
in the most pitiful perplexity, and consulted Dr.
Berry, of Wolverhampton. ' What would you do
if you were in my place ? ' he entreated. ' I don't
know, Jowett, I am not there, and you are not there
yet ! When have you to act ? ' ' On Friday,'
Dr. Jowett replied. ' Then,' answered Berry, ' you
will find your way perfectly clear on Friday !
The Lord will not fail you ! ' And, surely enough,
on Friday all was plain.

One of the very greatest and wisest of all Queen
Victoria's diplomatists has left it on record that it
became an inveterate habit of his mind never to

allow any opinion on any subject to crystallize until
it became necessary to arrive at a practical decision.
Give God time, and even when the knife flashes in
air the ram will be seen caught in the thicket !
Give God time, and even when Pharaoh's host is on
Israel's heels a path through the waters will suddenly
open ! Give God time, and when the bed of the
brook is dry Elijah shall hear the guiding voice !
Yes, the Kindly Light must be treated very patiently.

II

And very obediently ! This has never been
better put than in *Robinson Crusoe,* the story of
whose experiences is one of the finest religious
classics in our literature. We all recall the agony
of consternation into which he was thrown on dis-
covering that he was not alone on his island. The
presence of savages changed the outlook completely, and he knew not which way to turn. In
his confusion he sought the divine guidance, and in
language that has never been excelled by Quaker
or by mystic he tells at length of those secret hints
given to his spirit, directing him, in opposition to
his inclinations, to go this way or that way, by means
of which his life was preserved from a thousand
perils. To his instant and unquestioning response
to these ' secret hints and pressings of mind ' he

attributed everything.   The whole passage is worthy
of a careful reperusal.   It is a gem.

From Robinson Crusoe to Paul is not so far a cry
as it seems.   There is nothing in the New Testament
more dramatic than the great missionary's silent
journey across Asia.   He set his face towards the
evangelization of the stately commercial capitals
of the Eastern world.   But in each place he was
' forbidden of the Holy Ghost to preach the Word,
and trudged on in stillness.   ' The Spirit suffered
him not.'   As the Quakers would say, ' there was a
stop in his mind against it.'

> I hear a voice you cannot hear,
>   Which says I must not stay ;
> I see a hand you cannot see,
>   Which beckons me away.

And the result of Paul's implicit obedience to that
mysterious inward restraint was—EUROPE !   It
shifted the balance of power, and altered the face of
the world.   As Benjamin Kidd has demonstrated,
the great western empires sprang out of that extraordinary silence, that mystical submission.   It is
ever so.   Carey planned to evangelize the South
Seas.   The inward monitor said *India* !   Livingstone
selected China.   The voice said *Africa* !   And who
that realizes what Europe has meant to the world,

what Carey has meant to India, and what Livingstone has meant to Africa, shall doubt the wisdom
of unquestioning compliance with that secret
dictate? Yes, the Kindly Light must be treated
very obediently.

III

And very gratefully! For, however difficult it
may be to see the gleam leading on through the
gloom, it is never difficult, on looking back, to see
that we have been led. A brilliant essayist has said
that ' John Wesley was being trained for his mission
long before he appeared on this planet. The High
Churchmanship of his father, the Puritan strain
in his wonderful mother—were not these master-
elements in the forming of his soul? ' So early the
Kindly Light was leading ! With almost wearisome
monotony biographers point out to us the wonderful
way in which each separate phase of life peculiarly
fits a man for the next. To take a single illustration,
which is typical of scores, and which I select only
because of its conciseness, Sir Alfred Lyall, in his
Life of Lord Dufferin, remarks : ' The appointments
which he had previously held had been of such a
kind that if they had been purposely undertaken
as a course of preparatory training for the Indian
Viceroyalty, a more appropriate selection could

hardly have been made ! ' Similar instances might easily be multiplied. Sir W. Robertson Nicoll affirms that very few old men look back with regret upon the decisions that they made at the crises of their careers. ' The meaning of that is,' he adds significantly, ' that we are not left so much to our own wisdom as we think. All unconsciously to ourselves we have been guided.' The Kindly Light must be treated very gratefully.

' Up over my table,' writes that most fascinating personage the ' Lady of the Decoration,' ' I have a little picture that you sent me, matey, of the " lane that turned at last." You always said my lane would turn, and it *has*—into a broad road, bordered by cherry blossoms and wistaria.' We have most of us found, somewhere in life, just such an avenue of glorious blossom and delicious fragrance. And as we stroll amidst the loveliness of its petals and the luxury of its perfume, it will do us a world of good to bow our heads and to adore with thankful hearts the Kindly Light that led.

VI

A BUSH PHILOSOPHER

I HAVE just been out in the forest. It is fine to watch the woodman at his work. The plaintive swish of the swaying boughs ; the rhythmic thwack of the swinging axe ; the furious hail of the flying chips as the yawning gash grows greater ; and then, at last, the creak and the strain and the crash and the roar as the mighty monarch falls ! All this I saw and heard to-day as I read the prophet's vivid tale. And then I saw the hot and tired backwoodsman loll for a moment or two against the stump, surveying the humbled cedar, and wiping the beaded perspiration from his brow.

'What shall I do with it ? ' he asked himself, as he proudly eyed his hard-earned prize.

That is the question : ' *What shall I do with it ?* ' And it was the shrewd and systematic way in which he resolved that problem that made me reach for paper and pen. For, see ! he determines to divide the fallen tree into three parts. With the first part he will roast his meat. A man must eat ; and he

thus pays his tribute to the *necessities* of life. And
then he thinks of the chilly evening, after the sun has
set over the distant sea. He will have a blazing
camp-fire, and will warm himself, and will laugh and
say, ' Aha, I am warm ; I have seen the fire ! '
He thus makes his contribution to the *luxuries*
of life. And then from the remnant of his log he
will carve out for himself a god ; and he will fall
down to it, and worship it, and pray to it, and say,
' Save me, for thou art my god ! ' It is good to see
that he is not unmindful of the *sanctities* of life.
These three divisions are most fascinating. It is
worth while thridding the tortuous tracks of a mazy
Syrian forest to make the acquaintance of a horny-
handed philosopher like this !

Now, here is a subject for a painter's canvas !
The deep blue Syrian sky overhead ; the riot of
tangled forestry around ; the newly-fallen cedar ;
the fragrant chips scattered everywhere ; and the
exhausted axeman, perspiring and out of breath,
leaning against the stump arranging the disposition
of his prize. ' What shall I do with it ? ' he asks.
That is a picture drawn from real life. Indeed, it is
a picture drawn from every life. For we each of us
come to that moment sooner or later ; and everything—simply everything—depends upon the decision we then make We realize proudly that

something has become our own ; and we ask ourselves what we shall do with it now that we have
added it to our possessions. ' *What shall we do with
it ?* '—that is life's crucial question. There is no
earthly sense in everlastingly chopping down trees
unless we know what we propose to do with the
timber. There is no earthly sense in everlastingly
heaping up wealth unless we know what we propose
to do with the gold. I raise my hat respectfully to
this old idolater in the wilds of his Oriental forest,
and I only hope that I may be found to have paid
my dues to the necessities, the luxuries, and the
sanctities of life as well and as wisely as did he !
For, beyond the shred of a shadow of a shade of a
doubt, life consists, not in chopping down trees, but
in the discreet disposal of the timber when once we
have felled them.

My whole earthly fortune, my entire bag and
baggage, my complete stock-in-trade, may consist
of this tiny drop of ink that now trembles at the
point of my pen, and of this sheet of white paper
that lies spread out before me as I write. But that
matters little. Think of the possibilities that lie
before a sheet of paper and a drop of ink ! A poet
could set the world singing with that sheet of paper
and that drop of ink, and could impart to the fluttering folio a high commercial value. A millionaire

could scribble a few words upon that sheet of paper with that drop of ink that would make the page of equal value with all his hoarded millions. A statesman could, with that piece of paper and that drop of ink, write a declaration of war that would turn the world into a shambles. ' What a strangely potent, Protean thing a drop of ink may grow to be ! ' wrote Mr. George Wilson in a very early number of *Macmillan's Magazine*. ' Think of a Queen's first signature to a death-warrant, where tears tried to blanch the fatal blackness of the dooming ink ! Of a traitor's adhesion to a deed of rebellion, written in gall ! Of a forger's trembling imitation of another's writing, where each letter took the shape of the gallows ! Of a lover's passionate proposal, written in fire ! Of a proud girl's refusal, written in ice ! Of a mother's dying expostulation with a wayward son, written in her heart's blood ! Of an indignant father's disinheriting curse on his first-born, black with the lost colour of the grey hairs which shall go down in sorrow to the grave—think of these, and of all the other impassioned writings to which every hour gives birth, and what a strangely potent, Protean thing a drop of ink grows to be ! '

Now, a blind man can see what that means. For if it applies to drops of *ink*, it applies also to drops of *gold* ; aye, and to drops of *blood* ! For, see ! the log of cedar became divided into three parts—into necessities, into luxuries, into sanctities —*in exact proportion to the place held by these things in the heart of the woodman before the tree was felled.* That is the point.   The trembling drop of ink simply became the instrument by means of which the characters of the poet, the millionaire, the statesman, the monarch, the traitor, the forger, and the lover expressed themselves.   The ink becomes part of the life and soul and history of the man whose ink it is.   That is always so.   *Mine* becomes *me*.   I said that it applied, not only to drops of ink, but to drops of gold.   Is that not so?   See, I hold a sovereign in my hand.   It appears to bear the image and superscription of the King.   That is merely an optical illusion.   It bears *my own* image and superscription.   I have earned it, and it is mine.   But now that it is mine, the trouble begins.   For that sovereign becomes part of myself, and will henceforth represent a pound's worth of *me* !   If I am a bad man, I shall spend it in folly, and accelerate the forces that make for the world's undoing.   If I am a bad man, that is to say, it will be a bad sovereign, however truly it may seem to ring If I am a good man, I shall spend it in clean commerce, and enlist it among the forces that tend to the uplift of my brothers.   Yes, drops of gold are

very like drops of ink—and logs of cedar—in that
respect. They are very good if *we* are very good,
and very bad if *we* are very bad. Here is the song
of the sovereign :

> Dug from the mountain-side, washed in the glen,
> Servant am I or the master of men ·
> > Steal me, I curse you ;
> > Earn me, I bless you ;
> Grasp me and hoard me, a fiend shall possess you ;
> > Lie for me, die for me ;
> > Covet me, take me,
> Angel or devil, *I am what you make me* !

Mr. Ginterman is quite right. The log of cedar,
the drop of ink, the coin of gold, will be what we
make them. And since, by becoming our own, they
mix with the very fabric and substance of our being,
they will henceforth be what we are, and represent
ourselves, for what we are worth, among the high-
ways and byways of the world. Let every man
who would pursue this subject further, to his certain
and everlasting profit, procure forthwith a copy of
William Law's *Serious Call*, and read on his bended
knees that notable sixth chapter ' *containing the
great obligations, and the great advantages, of making
a wise and religious use of our estates and fortunes.*'
And if, before he rises, he reads on to the seventh
chapter and sees ' *how the imprudent use of an estate*

*corrupts all the tempers of the mind, and fills the heart
with poor and ridiculous passions, through the whole
course of life,'* it will be all the better for him.

I said just now that all this applies not only to
drops of ink and drops of gold, but to *drops of blood.*
That is actually so. ' The blood is the life.' Mr.
H. G. Wells, in *Marriage*, paints a very pitiful picture which exactly illustrates my point. His hero,
Trafford, a clever scientist, discovers the secret of
synthetic rubber. He sells it, making a large fortune. He soon finds himself the husband of a charming wife, the father of beautiful children, and the
possessor of a lovely home. Nothing that heart
could wish is denied him. But, somehow, all these
things merely accentuate life's deepest failure ;
and, looking round upon his wealth, he cries out
bitterly, ' What are we doing with it ? *What are
we doing with it ?* '

This leads us to the very crux of the problem.
It is a great moment when a man stands, not over
a log of cedar, or a drop of ink, or a bag of gold,
but with his very life in his hand, saying to himself,
' What shall I do with it ? ' Garrick, in Sir Joshua
Reynolds' famous picture, torn between tragedy and
comedy, is nothing to it. Who has not felt sorry for
Goethe, strolling in agony among the willows on
the banks of the Lahn, struggling vainly to decide

whether to be a lawyer or an artist? Or Lord
Dufferin as a young man in direst perplexity as
to whether to devote his life to poetry or politics?
Or Alfred Ainger, gazing wistfully at the beckoning
fingers of stage and law and church, and at his wits'
end as to which to follow? Or Frederick W.
Robertson, of Brighton, embarrassed between the
conflicting claims of the army and the pulpit? In
each case the man's course may seem clear enough
to us. It is so easy to be wise after the event. But
in each case it was a veritable Gethsemane to the
man himself. It is impossible to deny admiration
to the man who deliberately takes his life in his
hand, and asks himself the woodman's question.
So many of us are content to drift. We chop down
our trees and take our chance as to what becomes
of them.

There is only one thing in Isaiah's story of this
Syrian backwoodsman that I am sorry for. I
admire the way in which he divided his treasure
among the necessities, the luxuries, and the sanctities
of life. It was a fine thing to find room for the
sanctities. It is not everybody who does. But
I am sorry—very sorry—that he put the sanctities
last. He devoted the first part to cooking his food—
the *necessities* of life. And he devoted the second
part to the fire by which he laughed and rubbed his

hands in cheerful glee—the *luxuries* of life. And
the *residue* thereof—I don't like that!—he made
into an idol. I am sorry he only gave his leavings
to his god. But there! he was only an idolater
after all! And perhaps his god was only worthy of a
third place. But we are very differently circum-
stanced, and must be careful to put first things first.

The sister of Nietzsche tells us that, when the
thinker was a little boy, he and she once decided to
take each of them a toy to give to the Moravian
Sisters in support of their missionary enterprise
They carefully chose their toys and duly carried them
to the sisters. But when they returned Nietzsche
was restless and unhappy. His sister asked what
ailed him. ' I have done a very wicked thing,' the
boy answered. ' My fine box of cavalry is my
favourite toy and my best : I should have taken
that!' 'But do you think,' his sister asked, ' do
you think God always wants *our best* ? ' ' Yes,'
replied the young philosopher, ' always, *always*!'
The lad was then, at least, following a true instinct.
Professor William James, in his Lecture to Teachers
on ' The Stream of Consciousness,' says that every
object is either ' *focal* ' or ' *marginal* ' in the mind.
That represents with psychological precision the
difference between the sanctities of life as they
appeared to my Syrian bushman and the sanctities

of life as they appeared to the boy philosopher. In the one case they were merely marginal ; in the other they were grandly focal.   Surely, if they have a place at all, they should be in the very centre of the field—regal, transcendent, sublime.   The whole matter is summed up there.

VII

SPECTRE AND SONG

I

I CONFESS that I was puzzled. I had been reading
that chiefest and choicest gem of all devotional
literature—David's great penitential psalm, li., and
I had been arrested by this startling statement :
' *My sin is ever before me !* ' Now, when you come
to think of it, that is an awful thing.   To be haunted,
summer and winter, sleeping and waking, by that
ugliest and most hideous of all spectres, its ghostly
finger continually pointing relentlessly and accus-
ingly into the contrite penitent's face !   It was
with him in the night, and he drenched his pillow
with his tears.   It rose with him every morning.
It tracked him through every day.   His whole life
was a sob.   ' Ever before me !   Ever before me ! '
There can be no apparition, in fact or in fiction, so
fearfully frightful as that !   But I have not yet
stated the real cause of my perplexity.   It was
just this.   Even as this dreadful sentence was beat-
ing itself into my shuddering soul, it flashed upon

me that I had come upon it in the world's greatest
and grandest hymn-book—the Book of Psalms.
I had found this gruesome utterance in the very
heart of a burst of rapturous music. Now, here is
the riddle : How could it come about that this
man, whose life was haunted by his past transgres-
sion, was at the same time the blithest songster that
Israel ever knew ? How did it happen that this
man, with the hunted look in his eyes, with his
tear-drenched pillow, with his stricken conscience
and broken heart, was the gayest, happiest spirit
that the world has ever known ? Now, *there* was
the problem that baffled me as I sat with my
Bible on my knee—the incongruous conjunction of
misery and melody. It may have been a flight of
fancy that followed. I do not know. But I felt
that I should like to submit this puzzling discord
to the very highest authorities, and to sit humbly
at their feet whilst they pronounced upon it. But
to whom should I go ? I wanted the masters, not of
the *head*, but of the *heart*. At last I thought of the
twelve who companied with Jesus. But I could not
ask them all. And, besides, they did not all alike
impress me as being authorities on such a puzzle
of the inmost soul as that which baffled me. Then,
suddenly, I thought of that sacred triad which
Jesus formed from out of the twelve. Amidst the

glory of the holy mount, in the solemn stillness of the dead child's room, and in the dreadful anguish of Gethsemane, He took with Him James and Peter and John. These were His comrades and confidants. Perhaps *they* would know. I thought I asked them. And this is what they said.

II

I asked *James*. I told him that it seemed to me that David was haunted by a grim spectre that he could not lay even if he would, and that he would not lay even if he could. And yet how his whole heart sang! How was it? And I thought that the apostle answered me. David liked to have his sin ever before him—terrifying as the shocking apparition was—in order to keep fresh and sweet and warm within his soul the rapture of the divine forgiveness and the infinite tenderness of the divine love. Now, whether this conversation was a mere frolic of my fancy or not, that reply is worth thinking about. James could remember a time when he aspired to a lofty place in the Messiah's kingdom. He knew how easily the heart forgets the real treasures of the kingdom of heaven and hankers after baubles. And the man who has his sin eternally haunting him will never wander far from the wealthiest things. He will build his home near the

Cross. It is so easy for us ministers and officers and teachers to become superior and professional, and to forget that we were cleansed from our old sins. But the minister or officer or worker whose sin tracks him down as David's did, and stands, with ghostly accusing hand outstretched, perpetually before him, will clap his hands as he rises every morning for very joy that he is forgiven. As he eats his meals and does his work—his sin ever before him—all the bells of his heart will be ringing with holy merriment. He will preach because he cannot be quiet, and sing as the thrushes sing because it is easier to be songful than to be silent.

III

I asked *Peter*. I told him that it seemed so strange to me that David could be so terribly haunted and yet so tremendously happy at one and the same time. How was it? And I thought that Peter answered me. David liked to have his sin ever before him, in order to keep him wary and watchful, guarded and prayerful. And again I say, whether this conversation of mine was a mere freak of my fancy or not, that reply is worth turning over. Peter's memory lashed him sometimes most mercilessly. Could he ever forget that threefold denial and threefold absolution? Never! And

what then ? The horse that has once fallen may
easily tumble again ! The tiger that is tamed may
once more feel the old passion for blood ! The
snake that is charmed may yet show the force of its
fangs ! That is why Peter, in his epistles, had so
much to say about being *kept*. ' *Kept* by the power
of God.' Ah, yes ; Peter and David liked to have
their horrible, shameful, gruesome old sins ever
before them, that they might tremble one moment
and trust the next. Whilst such alarming memories
haunted them, they were incessantly on their guard
lest, peradventure, in a moment that they thought
not, like a thief in the night, the old tragedy recurred.

IV

I asked *John*. I told him that I was puzzled
by this singular juxtaposition of horrid spectre
and of happy song. How was it ? And I thought
that the beloved disciple answered me. David
liked to have his sin ever before him, and would
not lay that ghost, even if he could, in order that
he might be exceedingly tender, and charitable,
and compassionate, and sympathetic, in his treatment of others. And once more I say that, whether
this conversation of mine was a mere trick of my
imagination or not, that reply is worth a thought in
passing. David and John felt that it was the

delight of their lives that God had so wonderfully
forgiven them.   They felt that it was the *duty* of
their lives greatly to forgive others.   They therefore made it the *determination* of their lives never
to forgive themselves—to keep their sin ever before
them.   When John Wesley was re-crossing the
Atlantic on his return from his mission, he was
greatly troubled concerning his own unseemly
conduct and his unworthy conversation with his
fellow passengers on board.   He therefore resolved
' never to speak to any one who might oppose him,
or who might sin against God, without having all
his own sins set clearly in array before his face.'
When Livingstone was asked how he contrived to
treat the treachery and villany of African natives
and Arab traders with such infinite patience and
extraordinary calm, he quietly remarked, ' *I have
faults myself!* '   His own sin, ever before him,
gave him tender and charitable thoughts of others.
There is nothing like it, as David knew, and as John
knew, and as Wesley knew.   It was just because
his own sin was ever before him that David could
write his wonderful evangelistic psalms, giving
encouragement and hope to the vilest things creeping.   It was just because his own sin was ever
before him that John went down to his grave, in the
days of grey hairs, still repeating, ' My little children,

love one another ; love one another.' It was just because John Wesley's own sin was ever before him that the roughest men and the foulest women of England were made to feel the warm glow of his sympathy and the resistless power of his message. How can I harshly judge the guiltiest thing that breathes if my own sin is ever before me ? It is impossible !

V

I took the Bible from my knee, closed it, and laid it aside. I had seen daylight through my mystery. It is only those who know what it is to be haunted who know what it is to be happy The Spectre and the Song are inseparable.

VIII

THE PIONEER

EVERY Australian has reverently raised his hat at some time or other to Mr. McCubbin's great picture ' The Pioneer.' It holds a place of honour in the Melbourne Art Gallery, and copies of it have found their way into every home in the Commonwealth. I speak of it as a picture ; but it is really three pictures in one frame.

The first of the set represents the pioneer on pilgrimage. There stands the wagon ! The horses are turned out to forage for food among the scrub The man himself is making a fire under a giant blue-gum. And, in the very foreground, sits the sad young wife, her chin resting heavily upon her hand, and her elbow supported by her knee. Her dark eyes are eloquent with unspeakable wistfulness, and her countenance is clouded with something very like regret. Her face is turned from her husband lest he should read the secret of her sorrow, and see that her heart is breaking. She is overwhelmed by the vastness and loneliness of these great

Australian solitudes ; and her soul, like a homing bird, has flown back to those sweet English fields and fond familiar faces that seem such an eternity away across the wilds and the waters. The pioneer's wife !

The centre picture—the largest of the trio— shows us the freshly built home in the depths of the bush. The little house can just be seen through a rift in the forest. In the foreground is the pioneer. He is clearing his selection, and rests for a moment on a tree that he has felled. His axe is beside him, and the chips are all about. Before him stands his wife, with a little child in her arms. The soft baby-arm lies caressingly about her shoulders.

In the third picture we can see, through the trees, a town in the distance. In the immediate foreground is the pioneer. He alone figures in all three pictures. He is kneeling this time beside a rude wooden cross. It marks the spot among the trees where he sadly laid *her* to rest.

The pioneer ! It is by such sacrifices that these broad Australian lands of ours have been consecrated. Oh, the brave, brave women of our Australian bush ! We have heard, even in Tasmania, of their losing their reason through sheer loneliness ; and too often they have sunk into their graves with only a man to act as nurse and doctor

and minister and grave-digger all in one. George
Essex Evans has sung sadly enough :

The red sun robs their beauty, and, in weariness and pain,
The slow years steal the nameless grace that never comes
    again ;
And there are hours men cannot soothe, and words men
    cannot say—
The nearest woman's face may be a hundred miles away.

The wide bush holds the secrets of their longing and desires,
When the white stars in reverence light their holy altar fires,
And silence, like a touch of God, sinks deep into the breast—
Perchance He hears and understands the women of the West.

Yes ; there is a world of pathos and significance
in that solitary grave in the lonely bush. And he
who can catch that mystical meaning has read one
of life's deepest and profoundest secrets. He is not
very far from the kingdom of God !

I used to think that the finest thing on earth was
self-sacrifice. It was a great mistake. This picture
of ' The Pioneer ' reminds me that there is a form of
sacrifice compared with which *self*-sacrifice is a very
tame affair. I say that the picture *reminds* me ; for
it was the Bible that taught me of that sacrifice
supreme. Take two classical stories from the Old
Testament, both of which are recited in that glowing

chapter that Dr. Jowett calls 'the Westminster Abbey of the Bible'—the eleventh chapter of the Epistle to the Hebrews. The stories are those of Abraham's sacrifice of his son and Jephthah's sacrifice of his daughter—only children, both of them. What a small thing, in comparison with either of these sacrifices, *self*-sacrifice would have been ! Abraham would gladly have died a hundred deaths rather than have lifted the knife against 'his son, his only son Isaac.' And how cheerfully Jephthah would have gone to the altar if by so doing he could have saved his daughter ! There are few passages, even in the Bible, more charged with tender emotion than those two phrases, ' *Take now thy son, thine only son, Isaac, whom thou lovest,*' and ' *She was his only child : beside her he had neither son nor daughter.*'

I know that there are those who, like Principal Douglas, think that Jephthah did not slay his daughter upon the altar, but resigned her to a kind of convent life. As to that, there are only two things to be said. First of all, I cannot imagine that any one who has read Dr. Marcus Dods' monograph, or Dr. Alexander Whyte's lecture, or Dean Stanley's illuminating exposition, can hold that view. As Dean Stanley says, ' A more careful study of the Bible has brought us back to the original sense. And with it returns the deep pathos of the original

story, and the lesson which it reads of the heroism
of the father and the daughter, to be admired and
loved, in the midst of the fierce superstitions across
which it plays like a sunbeam on a stormy sea.'
And the second thing is that, for my present purpose,
it does not affect the argument. One of the most
touching letters in our literature is the letter written
by Lord Russell of Killowen, recently Lord Chief
Justice of England, to his daughter May, on her
resolving to enter a convent. ' My darling child,'
Lord Russell says, ' God's will be done ! It is a
terrible blow to your mother and me ! We hoped,
selfishly no doubt, to have your sunshiny nature
always with or near us in the world—a world in
which we thought, and think, good bright souls have
a great and useful work to do. Well, if it cannot be
so, we bow our heads in resignation. We have no
fear that you will forget us. After all, it is something
for us, poor dusty creatures of the world, with our
small, selfish concerns and little ambitions, to have
a stout young heart steadily praying for us. I know
we can depend on this. I know also that you will
not forget your promise to me, should serious mis-
givings cross your mind *before* the last word is
spoken. I rely on this. God keep and guard you,
my darling child, is the prayer of your father.' Nobody who has read Lord Russell's biography will

ever be seriously affected by the alternative presented in the case of Jephthah's daughter.

The point is that the sacrifice of one who is dearer
than life itself is manifestly a greater sacrifice than
self-sacrifice. It is such a sacrifice that Mr. McCubbin has painted. It is by such sacrifice that our
Australian scrub has been sanctified. It is made
as sacred as a shrine, and its sands more precious
than gold. We take off the shoes from off our feet,
for the place whereon we stand is holy ground.
And it is such a sacrifice, under either interpretation,
that Jephthah made. The Book of Maccabees
celebrates the virtues of that noble Jewish mother
who stood by whilst, one after another, her seven
sons were cruelly tormented and slain. As first one
and then another was tortured, she pleaded with
each, as he loved her, to suffer and die rather than
prove false to his father's faith. And the story of her
own martyrdom at the end of the chapter reads
quite tamely after the thrilling pageant that has
passed before. Her sacrifice of her seven sons, who
were more to her than her own flesh and blood, was
the sacrifice supreme. The sacrifice of *herself* seems
small in comparison. That is the lesson that I learn
as I gaze on Mr. McCubbin's picture. If only the
pioneer's struggles had led to *his own* death ! That
would have been a very little price to pay. But that

cross in the scrub ! Oh, yes, the pioneer knew, and Abraham knew, and Jephthah knew, and that noble Jewish woman knew, and Lord Russell of Killowen knew, that there is a sacrifice infinitely greater than *self*-sacrifice.

There lies before me an old copy of Foxe's *Book of Martyrs*. How we underrate many of these stories, as though the lions, or the stake, or the rack, represented the real torture ! *That* is merely self-sacrifice ; but there is a greater wonder here for those who have eyes anointed to see it. Here, for example, is the story of Perpetua, ordered, for being a Christian, to be thrown to wild beasts at Carthage. Perpetua was a young widow, aged twenty-six, with an infant child at her breast. Her aged father visited her in prison, and implored her on his knees, for the sake of his grey hairs, to make some offering to the Roman gods. Indeed, so passionate did he become in his frantic anxiety to save his daughter that he tried to carry her off, and received a staggering blow from one of the prison officers. Perpetua said that she felt that blow on her old father's head more than anything that she herself had suffered. Now, wherein lay the martyrdom of Perpetua ? The pictures would have us believe that it consisted in being torn to pieces by wild beasts. I do not believe it. That is mere *self*-sacrifice. The sacrifice supreme was made when she kissed her baby for the last time, and threw her arms about the bowed and broken form of her father, whose old age she was leaving comfortless. It cost poor Perpetua little to sacrifice *herself*, but it broke her heart to sacrifice *their* happiness and welfare.

Now these two—Perpetua's aged father and Perpetua's little babe—are representative characters. They are like symbols, emblems, types. They stand for a great deal. I have seen a young missionary's face blanch as he looked towards a horrid climate steaming with fever and malaria. But the agony was not for himself. It was as easy to die among those pestilential bogs and swamps as anywhere else. But what of the old folks at home? Here is Perpetua's father over again! We remember how, when W. C. Burns set out for China in 1846, his mother found it so hard to part with him, that, after walking some distance with him from the old homestead, she seemed unable to endure any longer the intensity of her emotion, and giving him a vigorous push, said: 'There, noo, I've gi'en thee to the Lord! Go!' It is that kind of thing that makes the departure so hard. It is the problem of Perpetua's father.

Perpetua's child, too; I think I have seen its counterpart. What of Livingstone and his family in the desert ? He saw his children dying of fearful thirst under his very eyes. ' The agony of it,' Mr. Silvester Horne says, ' must have nearly killed him.' ' The less there was of water, the more thirsty,' Livingstone says, ' the little rogues became. The idea of their perishing was terrible ! ' Here is the anguish of the pioneer ! What is self-sacrifice compared with this ? And that little grave in the desert where they buried the baby ! ' Hers,' says the father, ' was the first grave in all that country marked as the resting-place of one of whom it is believed and confessed that she shall live again ! ' As I stand beside this little tomb in Central Africa, I am back once more with Perpetua saying good-bye to the child of her bosom. This, surely, is the sacrifice supreme. And then I see Livingstone digging with his own hands that other grave under the great baobab-tree at Shupanga, and moaning, ' Oh, Mary, Mary, my Mary ! I loved you when I married you, and the longer I lived with you the more I loved you ! ' And when I reverently gaze upon this, I look again at Mr. McCubbin's third picture— the pioneer kneeling by the lonely cross—and I fancy that I am not far from the very heart of things.

History and experience abound with instances of this sacrifice that is greater than self-sacrifice. In his autobiography Dr. Thomas Guthrie tells of a visit

paid him by the great Dr. McCrie, the historian of
John Knox. ' My second son, James,' says Dr.
Guthrie, ' was then an infant in the nurse's arms, and
I distinctly remember the great and good man taking
him in his arms, and saying, as he held out the child
to me, and in allusion to the martyrdom of that
other James Guthrie, the Covenanter, " Would you
be willing that *this* James Guthrie should suffer, as
the other did, for the Church of Christ ? " ' And
later on, in the great Disruption days, the scene came
back with poignant force to the memory of Dr.
Guthrie. For when the ministers left their kirks
and manses for conscience' sake, it was the wives
and children that suffered most. In one home—
' a home that had known many cradles and many
coffins, and in which every flower and shrub and tree
was dear to them '—Guthrie heard, through the
partition, the moaning of the minister's wife.
' That woman's heart was like to break ! ' ' In
another locality,' he says, ' there was a venerable
mother who had gone to the place when it was a
wilderness, but who, with her husband, had turned
it into an Eden. Her husband had died there.
Her son was now the minister. She herself was
eighty years of age. When I looked upon her aged
head, white with many snows and sorrows, I felt that
it was a cruel thing to tear her from the house that

was dearest to her on earth.' Yes ; the sacrifice of
the Disruption ministers was far more than self-
sacrifice. It was the sacrifice of children and wives
and mothers like these. They went out to starve
on the moors and hillsides of Scotland with such
heartrending cries in their ears. That was the
sacrifice supreme.

And so, as I turn again to Mr. McCubbin's painting, I seem to be looking, not at a picture, not at
three pictures, but at a gallery. For there are
others, companion pictures, ranging themselves
about it. A picture of Abraham standing beside
the prostrate form of ' his son, his only son, Isaac.'
A picture of Jephthah offering his daughter on the
altar in the valley. A picture of the noble Jewish
matron and her seven heroic sons. A picture of
Perpetua and her tearful farewell to her infirm
father and her clinging babe. A picture of Livingstone in his anguish beneath the great baobab-tree.
A picture of the Disruption ministers going out into
the unknown accompanied by weeping women and
hungry children. A picture of John Bunyan, too,
kissing, before going to Bedford Jail, the upturned
face of his sightless girl. ' Poor child ! how hard it
is like to go with thee in this world ! Thou must
be beaten ; must suffer hunger, cold, and nakedness ;
and yet I cannot endure that even the wind should

blow upon thee ! ' Here is a stately gallery ! A
glorious company this, a goodly fellowship, a noble
army of testifiers !

And as I still gaze at this great gallery, all the
pictures, including Mr. McCubbin's picture, seem to
range themselves around one great central canvas.
I said just now that, as I turned from the scene
beside Mary Livingstone's grave, and from the picture of the pioneer beside the lonely cross, I felt
that I was not far from the heart of things.   For
surely these sacrifices—each of them infinitely
greater than *self*-sacrifice—are but faint radiations
and dim reflections of the love that is everlasting,
the Sacrifice Supreme!   God so loved the world that
He gave His only-begotten Son ! *Gave His Only
Son !* GOD GAVE HIS SON !   All these sacrifices
that are greater than *self*-sacrifice point steadily up
to *that* !   We may leave the gallery now, and we
shall leave it with bowed heads !

IX

THE EXHILARATIONS OF LIFE

LIFE breaks down first of all on the side of its exhilarations. '*They have no wine!*' said Mary at the feast in Cana of Galilee. And she might say it still. It is life's first point of collapse. Health holds out. Money increases. Friends multiply. We have abundance to eat, plenty to drink, and warm beds to sleep in. But the wine fails. Life somehow loses its sparkle and its sprightliness. The gaiety and the elasticity depart. An eminent art critic stood before a picture. 'Yes,' he said, 'it is very good; but it lacks *that*'—expressively snapping his fingers. Every man discovers sooner or later that he lacks '*that.*'

Here are a pair of illustrations picked at random. The first is from Mrs. Barclay's *Mistress of Shenstone.* 'Yes,' replied Jim Airth, 'seven o'clock on the first of June I stood at the smoking-room window, *at a loose end of all things*; sick of myself, dissatisfied with my work, tired of everything.' The second is from one of Madeline Cope's beautiful letters in M. E.

Waller's *Woodcarver of 'Lympus*. ' Before I knew
it, Hugh,' she says, ' I was dragging anchor, losing
the dear, sweet, childlike faith I had kept as my best
heritage from my father and mother, and, with it,
losing much of *the spontaneous joy of life*.' That is it
exactly. ' Dragging anchor.' ' Losing the spontaneous joy of life.' ' They have no wine ! ' The
vim and the vivacity have vanished. Not that we
become positively miserable. No. There are no
tears. It does not rain. The sun merely hides
itself behind dense clouds. The birds hush themselves into sullen silence. The song dies from the
lips. Life becomes sombre and grey. That loss
of sunshine is, I repeat, the first breakdown that most
lives know. They do not become morbid or melancholy. They simply lose the exquisite exhilaration
of life. Laughter, which used to burst out like a
sparkling spring on a grassy hillside, has now to be
forced, like the tainted dribble of a rusty pump.
It is no longer a luxury to be alive. ' They have no
wine ! ' That is all. And it is quite enough.

For it is not too much to say that the whole of a
man's life takes its tone and colour from his behavi-
our at this crisis. ' Before you have finished,' said
Myrtle Reed's old violin-master to his young pupil,
' before you have finished, the world will do one
of three things with you. It will make your heart

very hard, it will make it *very soft*, or else it will *break it*. No one escapes ! ' Precisely ! That is literally so. No one escapes. And the world usually makes up its mind as to which of these three things it will do with a man when it sees what course he himself pursues when exhilarations fail—when the wine runs out. For at that critical juncture three roads meet. Exhilarations fail ; and a man makes up his mind to do without. That is the *first* possibility. He simply reconciles himself to grey days. He defiantly sets his teeth, and clenches his fist, and vows that he will see the horrid thing through. He becomes cynical, taciturn, sour. That is what the old violin-master meant when he said that the world may make your heart very hard. Or, at the other extreme, there is a *second* alternative. A man may do as Mary did. ' When they lacked wine, she said unto *Him*, They have no wine ! ' There is no wisdom in the heavens above nor on the earth beneath that can compare with that. Surely that was what the old music-master meant when he said, ' or it will make your heart very soft ! ' But there is the third course. A man may seek compensations. True, he feels that he has lost the sunshine. But what of that ? Are there no other lights ? True, the birds no longer sing. But what then ? Is there no other music ? He seeks in

ribald revelry to forget the finer flavour of that wine
that he may drink no more. Along that road he finds
disappointment, disillusionment, and heartbreak at
the last.   Yes ; the violin-master was quite right.
' Before you have finished, the world will do one of
three things with you.   It will make your heart very
hard, very soft, or else break it.   No one escapes ! '

We come to places at which the world treats us
as it treated Livingstone's native comrades.   We all
remember their sensation when, at Loanda, those
Central Africans saw the sea for the first time.
' We marched along with our father (Livingstone),'
they tell us, ' believing that what the Ancients had
always told us was true, that the world had no end.
But all at once the world said to us, " *I am finished,
there is no more of me ! " '*   Here is the point of exhaustion ; and it is around that very experience, in
another realm, that some of the most affecting
passages in our literature gather.   The world has
come to an end.   The wine has failed ; and the
heart has sought desperately, and in vain, for its
lost exhilaration

I cite two witnesses—George Fox, the founder of
the Quakers, and Cardinal Newman.   In most
respects the two men stand in striking and dramatic
contrast.   History can scarcely present two more
clear-cut variations.   But, just on that account,

The Exhilarations of Life 91

their evidence is the more valuable to us as we watch
their divergent experiences converge upon this
crucial point. Everybody who has read Mr. A. C.
Bickley's great biography of Fox will recall the
passages that describe, in effect, the failure of the
wine. It happened when he was at the age of
twenty ; and his experience was so pathetic and so
bitter as to move the compassion of both Macaulay
and Carlyle. ' Wherever he went,' Mr. Bickley tells
us, ' people pitied the gentle melancholy youth,
and many were anxious to befriend him. While
at Barnet, he was almost in despair, and he spent
many hours walking up and down in the Chace,
solitary and sad, trying to find some relief.' Here
he is, then ; this youth of twenty, who feels that the
wine has failed, and that life is left to him without
gaiety. He is ' trying to find some relief.' Let us
follow him in his search. ' One jolly old clergyman,'
says Macaulay, ' told him to smoke tobacco and sing
psalms ; another counselled him to go and lose some
blood. From these advisers the young inquirer
turned in disgust to the dissenters, and found them
also blind guides.' ' The clergy of the neighbourhood,' says Carlyle in *Sartor Resartus*, ' listened
with unaffected tedium to his consultations, and
advised him, as the solution of such doubts, *to drink
beer and dance with the girls* ! '

In the story of the Cardinal there is a pitiful
piece of correspondence between Newman and his
mother. The earnest young student writes to his
parents, telling of his doubts and fears and spiritual
struggles. It is clear that the wine has failed.
But the tragedy occurs, not in Newman's plaintive
letters to his mother, but in her reply to him. ' Your
father and I fear very much from the tone of your
letters that you are depressed. We fear you debar
yourself *a proper quantity of wine.*'

Now, here are two young men—historic figures
both of them. Both have felt life's first collapse, the
failure of the wine. Both have reached, in consequence, the crisis from which all subsequent experience takes its colour. And both are pointed down
the wrong road by those to whom they are entitled
to look for guidance. It would be easy to devote my
remaining space to an impressive application of a
very obvious moral to all parents and pastors. But
that would be beside my present mark.

' *Drink beer !* ' said the old clergyman to young
George Fox. ' *Take wine !* ' said Mrs. Newman to
her brilliant son. These are the pitiful expedients
that blind guides prescribe for aching hearts ! Beer
and wine ! Beer for Fox and wine for Newman !
Think of it ! What a lurid light is thrown by these
incidents upon our colossal national drink bill !

I cannot now contemplate these hundreds of thousands of pounds being spent throughout the Empire every year on beer and wine without conjuring up before my fancy millions of spiritual tragedies. Here are mystics of the measure of Fox, and thinkers of the type of Newman, painfully conscious that life's innermost exhilarations have failed them, seeking frantically to assuage their soul's intense desire by drinking beer and wine ! It is a spectacle for men and angels ! There are some aspects of the temperance question that provoke the passion of an orator ; this aspect appeals to emotions that do lie too deep for tears. It is the old, sad blunder. ' Soul, thou hast much goods laid up ! ' As though a man could feed his *soul* on corn ! As though the soul of Fox could be brightened by beer ! As though the soul of Newman could be exhilarated by any earthly vintage !

No, no, no ! It will not do ! There is a more excellent way. And Mary knew it. ' She saith unto *Him*, They have no wine.' Even Nature gives mysterious and subtle hints of perennial exhilarations rushing out of apparent exhaustions. Here is an illustration offhand. I have beside me two lectures. One is by Sir William Ramsay, K.C.B., of London, on ' British Coal Supply.' The other is by Professor Soddy, of Glasgow, on ' The Interpretation of Radium.' Sir W. Ramsay's lecture is really

on ' Exhaustion.' Professor Soddy's is really on
' Exhilaration.' Sir W. Ramsay says that coal is
the one source of energy to the British people. It
is by means of coal, he argues, that all our manifold
activities are sustained. But the coal-fields of the
United Kingdom, he tells us, will only last for 175
years. That is decidedly depressing. But listen to
Professor Soddy. ' The revelations of radium,'
he says, ' have shown that the world is not, as had
been supposed, slowly dying from exhaustion, but
bears within itself its own means of regeneration,
so that it may continue to exist in much the same
physical condition as at present for thousands of
millions of years.'

It is a parable. God has set His wonderful exhilarations over against our pitiful exhaustions.
Every student of history knows that Jesus came
into an exhausted world. Its ancient civilizations
were all played out. Like a clock, the whole thing
was in danger of running down. As Matthew
Arnold says, in ' Obermann,'

> On that hard pagan world disgust
>   And secret loathing fell ;
> Deep weariness and sated lust
>   Made human life a hell.

Then Jesus came, and changed the face of everything.

And in Him the nations found a fresh exhilaration. Here, surely, is a gospel worthy of our most persuasive powers ! What an invigorating and exhilarating thing a conversion really is ! I have just read Mr. Edward Smith's *Mending Men*. Here are men of wasted lives, jaded powers, flagging forces, dissipated energies, and depleted moral resources. Life was exhausted at every point. ' They had no wine.' Then into those beggared and bankrupt lives Jesus came. They were converted. And exhilarated ! Like the prodigal, they began to be merry. That is always the way. Dr. Campbell Morgan provoked a smile the other day by rendering the classic phrase of Habakkuk in this way : ' *I will jump for joy in the Lord ; I will spin round with delight in the God of my salvation.*' I have no doubt that the Principal of Cheshunt's translation is sound. I am quite sure that it is true to the facts of spiritual experience. Religion is a revelry.

> Heaven above is softer blue,
>   Earth around is sweeter green,
> Something lives in every hue
>   Christless eyes have never seen.
> Birds with gladder songs o'erflow,
>   Flowers with richer beauties shine,
> While I know, as now I know,
>   I am His, and He is mine.

Any man who has once discovered what a brave and bracing thing a conversion really is will be hungry to witness another. The beautiful phenomenon will fascinate him, and, like Mary, he will sadly look on an exhausted humanity, and say to his Lord, ' They have no wine ! ' And he will be restless and ill at ease until the vessels are filled to the brim.

PART II

I

THAT BLESSED WORD—' WHICH ? '

I RECENTLY enjoyed a very pleasant holiday. In the course of my travels I met with many ministers, and therefore heard many good stories. One of them has stuck to me. It was told me one hot night in the course of a quiet stroll across a sequestered park near Melbourne. Wild horses shall not drag from me the name of the teller of the tale. It may, however, impart to the narrative both the odour of sanctity and the hall-mark of authenticity if I merely mention the abstract circumstance that my informant is the grave and revered principal of a theological seminary. But to the story :

' I've been thanking the good Lord all day long for that blessed word " WHICH ? " ' said John to his friend.

' That blessed word " WHICH ? " ' replied his astonished companion. ' What on earth do you mean ? '

' Well,' explained John, ' it's like this. For many years I gave way to drink. Our home was a poor sort of place. My Mary hadn't a very nice life of it. But she bore it all like a saint, and never murmured. And in those days I had no clothes except those I stood up in. But last year I started going to church with my Mary. And one night I was converted. And my, the difference it made! Why, last night my Mary was upstairs, and I called out to her to bring my clothes down when she came. And what do you think she called back? She shouted " WHICH ? " And, oh, it made me feel good to hear my Mary ask me that! And I've been thanking the good Lord all day for that blessed word " WHICH ? " '

I brought back many good things from my holiday, but I cherish this choice gem among the richest of my treasures. It is delicious. And now that I pick it up more leisurely and examine it more closely, I am not surprised that it was given me by a Professor of Divinity. If he can contrive to pack as much sound and sparkling philosophy into as little space in the course of all his lectures to his students, we shall expect a generation of ministerial prodigies to invade our pulpits as they issue from beneath his care.

' WHICH ? ' Shall it be the grey suit or the black suit ?—that is the all-absorbing question. That is the fine point which the faithful Mary submits to her happy lord. And her ' WHICH ? ' as she calls down the stairs, sets him chuckling and crooning to himself for many hours afterwards,—' that blessed word " WHICH ? " '

John's wardrobe, with its two suits, is a fitting emblem of the world in general, and of my own individual world in particular. John cannot wear both suits at once, but it is lovely to have them both to choose from. Life is full of margins, of surpluses, of overflows. We rarely get one thing dumped down to us with no choice, no selection, no alternative. I find myself surrounded at every turn by a wonderful, and sometimes embarrassing, profusion. My butcher calls every morning for orders, and the very fact that he finds it necessary to call for my order proves that I am confronted by a wide choice of viands. I daresay I could live on beef if there were no other meat in the universe. But there *are* other meats, and I have my choice. I cannot have everything that he has in stock ; I do not need everything ; I do not like everything. But I like him to greet me every morning with ' that blessed word— " WHICH ? " ' It makes me feel that I am living in a wealthy world. Or suppose that I fancy a little fruit. See what happens at once ! All the gardens and orchards of the world stretch out their hands to me. I fancy I should love this old earth of ours a little less if she said to me, ' I can only produce bananas ! ' or ' I only grow peaches ! ' In that case, being a cross-grained and ill-tempered creature, I should probably sulk, and tell her that I did not want her old bananas, or that she could keep her peaches for herself. But the dear old earth never treats me like that. She treats me just as Mary treated John. She calls out ' that blessed word " WHICH ? " ' Any one kind of fruit would prob- ably satisfy the actual requirements of my physical make-up. But Nature does not consider that. She is never niggardly. She is ' my Lady Bounti- ful.' She heaps my table with apples and pears, plums and apricots, cherries and peaches, and then smilingly greets me with ' that blessed word " WHICH ? " ' I don't know what other worlds are like, but I know for certain that this is a good one.

Now, the beauty of it is that it does not matter a brass farthing to John, to Mary, or to anyone else which suit John decides to wear. Mary will walk just as proudly by his side whether he decides on the black or the grey. And the world will go round in pretty much the same way whichever garments John elects to don. But that isn't the point. The point is that the glorious possession of two suits—the black *and* the grey—gives John the precious privilege of choosing—the black *or* the grey. And the rapture

of choosing is one of life's lordliest luxuries.   What
a day that was when we strutted into a shop with our
very first sixpence, to spend it just as we liked !
Yes, a man dearly loves to choose.   It may be perfectly true that John looks best in black.   But even
then he does not relish having a black suit handed
to him by his dutiful Mary, and to be told that he
must wear *that*—that and no other.   He loves to be
asked, ' Grey or black ? ' even though he instantly
decides on black.   ' That blessed word " WHICH ? " '
appeals to a very subtle but very responsive chord
in the complexity of our wonderful composition.

I overheard two men chatting on a tramcar the
other afternoon.   They had just arrived from
England, and were discussing the trip.   One had
travelled second-class ; the other had come steerage.
They compared notes, and, being Englishmen, talked
much of the table.   The difference, so far as I could
make out, was simply this : In the second saloon
the steward came to the passenger and asked him if
he would take beef, mutton, or pork.   Whereas in
the steerage one or the other of these things was
placed in front of the passenger without a question
as to whether or not he would prefer something else.
The food in the steerage was just as good as in the
saloon ; and, as a matter of fact, the passenger in
the saloon did not care a snap of the finger whether

he had beef or mutton or pork ; but it tickled his
vanity to be offered a selection.   In the saloon they
sat down to dinner to the pleasing music of ' that
blessed word " WHICH ? " '   In the steerage that
charming melody was never heard.

I have just read Dan Crawford's *Thinking Black*.
And he says some striking things that may help us at
this very point.   He tells us, for example, that the
real inwardness of a native's horror of slavery consists in the consequent loss of the luxury of choosing.
Mr. Crawford translates for us a Bantu rhyme which
runs like this :

> As a bird in the course of its flight
> On some branch will not choose to alight,
>   For it likes not the tree,
> So man's heart doth resemble a bird,
> To coerce it would be as absurd,
>   For the heart must be free !

A slave may possibly become the property of a
most considerate and indulgent owner.   But it makes
little difference.   He is still a slave, a chattel, a possession ; he is not free.   His owner may give him
congenial work, and delicate food, and ample leisure.
But it does not count.   His spirit is crushed by the
feeling that he has no choice.   He cannot say to himself, ' I will do this,' or ' I will do that.'   He cannot

say, ' I will go here,' or ' I will go there.' The under-
lying agony and humiliation of slavery, even at its
best, is that it robs a man of that music for which his
very soul hungers, the music of ' that blessed word
" Which ? " '

I repeat that for that music his very soul hungers.
In His infinite and inscrutable wisdom God has left
room in human nature for the entertainment of fads
and whims, foibles and fancies. He has woven into
the wonderful web of our being an uncanny faculty
for liking without knowing why we like, and of detest-
ing without knowing why we abhor.

> I do not like you, Doctor Fell ;
> The reason why I cannot tell,
> But this I know and know full well,
> I do not like you, Doctor Fell !

And, just because we find ourselves possessed of
this weird and wayward faculty, we glory in choosing.
The grey suit may be just as good as the black suit ;
beef may be just as nice as mutton ; coffee may be
just as pleasant as tea. But we like to have our
choice. We are quite prepared to pay a little more
to travel saloon. We feel that we are next door to
slavery if we *must* wear this, or *must* eat that. We
dance through life to the delightful music of ' that
blessed word " Which ? " '

But to all this there are limits, and they are very stern and severe ones. We are allowed to choose between the grey suit and the black one because, after all, it really does not matter which we wear, and it pleases us to have our choice. We are permitted in the same way, and for the same reason, to choose between beef and mutton, between tea and coffee, between apples and pears. We simply cannot go wrong, and the luxury of selection adds a new piquancy to our pleasure. But there are things in which we *may* go wrong, and in which, therefore, we have no choice. We talk a great deal about ' choosing a husband ' and ' choosing a wife,' but I doubt if it ever works out that way. When a man falls in love with a woman, he sees her face in all the flowers, and every bird is singing her name. Choice is absurd ; there is only one woman in the universe after that. And certainly there are other things about which we have no option. The Ten Commandments, for example. There is no choice here ; no hint of an alternative ; no faintest whisper of ' that blessed word " WHICH ? " ' ' I am the Lord thy God,' says the very first of them. ' Thou shalt have no other gods but Me.' A man is not free to pick a deity or choose a god after that. And the mandates that follow adopt the same regal note. They present no alternatives ; they ask no favours ;

they offer no advice. *'Thou shalt. . . .'* *'Thou shalt not. . . .'* No man is free to choose his morals. In small matters in which we cannot go wrong, we have our choice. But in the big things, on which we might easily make shipwreck, we are left without an option. And most of all is this the case when it comes to the matter of the soul and its salvation. ' There is *none other Name* under heaven given among men whereby we must be saved.' We are shut up here, without choice or alternative. Jesus stands in splendid solitude as the one and only Saviour. And I, in entrusting my poor soul to Him, feel glad to relinquish, in this august instance, my native passion for picking and choosing.

II

THE BUILDING OF THE BRIDGE

MY paper this morning contains a cablegram from England announcing the death of Sir William Arrol, the peerless prince of bridge-builders. And, since reading the tale of his audacious undertakings and bewildering achievements, it has dawned upon me that bridge-building is the only profession worth following ! It is a lovely thing to see life's deep ravines—its raging torrents, its yawning abysses, its perilous chasms—and to fling across them bridges by which a little child may cross in safety. When I come to think of it, it really seems to me that we are sent into this old world of ours for no other purpose than to build bridges. Deep down in the mystery of our complex and wonderful nature there is a passionate yearning to span life's chasms. The instincts of the bridge-builder surge in our very veins, and sooner or later, in some form or other, they will certainly betray themselves.

Now, a chasm is always a tantalizing affair. Even when we were children, playing, on those long and lazy summer Saturdays, beside the babbling trout stream, as it meandered through the meadows, how wistfully we gazed at the willows, the hazels, and the blackberries on the opposite bank! As a matter of fact, there was nothing on that side that did not grow just as profusely on our own. But there it was! And as we fished and frolicked on our side of the flashing stream, the opposite bank teased our fancy and tortured our imagination. The very laughter of the rippling waters seemed to mock our inability to cross. And then, on one unforgettable holiday, there came a crowded hour of glorious life in which, at the hazard of our lives, we actually crossed the taunting waters. And who shall describe the rapture that flushed our faces, and ran down through all our blood, when we found ourselves romping among the buttercups, the daffodils, and the cowslips on that other bank? How every nerve tingled with triumph! The landing of Columbus on American soil was not effected amidst wilder transports of delight than were ours at that tremendous moment. With what proud and rapturous disdain we looked back upon the familiar commonplaces on our own side of the stream! What did it all mean? It simply meant that we had tasted, perhaps for the very first time, the joy of the bridge-builder.

And, after all, Columbus had done no more. We

have all followed Prescott's thrilling story of the young Italian's anguish as he gazed across the wild Atlantic waters at the world of which he had dreamed, but saw no way of reaching it. It was precisely the same poignant emotion, on a slightly larger scale, which we schoolboys experienced as we looked across the English trout-stream. And what was that adventurous and epoch-making voyage across uncharted seas, with black tempest roaring around and blacker mutiny raging aboard, but the construction of a bridge between the eastern and western hemispheres ? Bancroft opens his immense *History of the United States* with this sentence : ' The enterprise of Columbus—the most memorable maritime enterprise in the history of the world— formed between Europe and America the communication which will never cease.' That is to say, he built a bridge, and built it well. And what was Captain Cook but the builder of a bridge between the northern and southern hemispheres ? By means of those thrilling and romantic voyages he spanned the terrific chasm that yawned for countless centuries between the old world on the one bank and all the continents and islands of these southern seas on the other. Columbus and Cook were bridge-builders. That is all.

That is always the case. The explorer, whether

on sea or land, whether at the Pole or the Equator, is a master-builder of bridges. And we applaud him so enthusiastically because he appeals so directly to that subtle longing that in boyhood made us yearn for the other side of the sparkling stream. We love to be linked up. We like to feel that we are in touch with everything. A child glories in pictures of red men, and yellow men, and olive men, and bronze men, and brown men, and black men ; and he loves to feel that there are ships and trains by which these strange people can be reached. He collects postage stamps simply because they bring him into touch with all the remotest cracks and corners of civilization. He throws up his cap to welcome the swallows in the springtime because they have seen such strange things since he saw them in the autumn. They link him up with the people of some semi-tropical clime among whom they last made their homes. And, if I cared to labour the point, I could easily show that all our modern inventions—our telephones and telegrams, our mammoth liners and flying expresses, our Marconigrams and aeroplanes—are simply bridges, all of them, and we appreciate them so highly because they span our chasms so effectively. And what is language itself but the cunning contrivance by which we bridge the gulf that would otherwise yawn between one human soul and another ?

For there are chasms much more difficult to span than those represented by yards and furlongs and miles. What about those that are represented by months and years and centuries? How would the genius of Sir William Arrol grapple with that problem? Here am I, for example, in the twentieth century. I seem to be on an island. Across there to the left I see the nineteenth and eighteenth and seventeenth centuries—and crowds of others. Away to the right I see the twenty-first, twenty-second, and twenty-third centuries—and crowds of others. Now, my soul rebels against being cooped up in the century in which, by the veriest accident, I happened to be born. I want to get into communication with all sorts and conditions of men, some of whom were born a thousand years ago, and some of whom may not be born for a thousand years to come. You put the telephone into my study so that I can ring up my friends for miles around. You give me penny postage so that I can send a message to the most outlandish wilds. But what on earth is the good of all this unless you are prepared to carry the thing to its logical conclusion? I often want to ring up some old friend of mine in the Stone Age that was, or in the Golden Age that will be. It is ridiculous to bridge my geographical chasms unless you are prepared to bridge my chronological chasms as well.

I protest against such scamped work. It is a farce and a mockery. If you doom me to be imprisoned on this lonely little island that you are pleased to call the Twentieth Century, you may as well turn me into a Robinson Crusoe and have done with it. This isolation in a single period, with boundless other periods in sight, is frightful. It is galling beyond endurance. It is maddening. By hook or by crook you must bridge for me this terrible and tantalizing gulf.

Now, let nobody suppose that I am giving rein to my imagination. I am doing nothing of the kind. The desire to span that exasperating chasm between one age and another is one of the most passionate, and one of the most pathetic, in human history. A bird feels that it is the child of the forest and the heir of the skies ; and if you imprison it in a cage it will dash itself to pieces against the cruel bars. A man feels that he is the child of eternity and the heir of all the ages ; and if you shut him up in a single period, each year of which is like one bar in the terrible cage that has entrapped him, he will fret and chafe in mortal agony. Let me show how he contrives to escape.

I was motoring the other day across this beautiful island on which my lot is cast. In the course of that lovely autumn afternoon we came suddenly

upon a tiny cemetery. It was in the most out-of-
the-way spot, surrounded by a panorama of green
hills and graceful forestry. There was not a house
in sight. Yet in this lonely little God's acre there
stood several immense monuments, and, as the
westering sun fell athwart them, their long, gaunt
shadows stole along the grass like huge spectral
fingers pointing mutely but with wondrous meaning to the east, to the sunrise, to the hope of resurrec-
tion. These stately obelisks had been reared, at a
cost that represented no small sacrifice by men and
women who lived fifty years ago, and in the rude
inscriptions they celebrated the virtues of the men
and women of the generation before their own. And
here stood I, who was not born till long after these
village forefathers had died, reading their simple
story in the stones on this delightful autumn afternoon. These folk of fifty years ago felt the tyranny
of time. And they determined to build a bridge
that should connect the period in which their
honoured fathers lived with that in which unborn
generations should find themselves. And here was
I standing on that very bridge, and finding my life
linked up with the lives of men and women who
died before I was born, and whose epitaphs would
still be read after I had passed away. Surely that
is very beautiful! Or take another case.

Near to one of the great English universities is a bluff that commands a magnificent outlook across the charming country stretching away and away to the distant sunlit hills.   On the summit of the bluff is a stone seat.   And on the back of the rough stone bench is carved this legend :

TO THOSE WHO SHALL SIT HERE REJOICING,
AND
TO THOSE WHO SHALL SIT HERE LAMENTING ;
GREETING AND SYMPATHY !
SO HAVE WE DONE IN OUR TIME.

Here are students whose faces are flushed with success, and students whose lips quiver with the bitterness of failure, both of whom feel that in their hours of exaltation and of humiliation they must span the terrible gulf that separates them from similar students yet unborn.   And, by means of this rough stone bench upon the bluff, they fling a bridge across the chasm of time, and put themselves into communication with students who shall pass their examinations, and students who shall fail their examinations, long after the moss and the mildew have gathered about their own tombstones.

I have been greatly impressed lately by the touching concern that dying men display, under certain conditions, to keep their journals intact to the last

Think of Livingstone's Journal with its last records, written in extreme agony and mortal weakness, scarcely legible ! Think of Burke's Journal, written in the dusty heart of Australia, in which the dying explorer, so anxious that his record should be complete, carries it right down to the moment when he stretched his exhausted form upon the desert sands and gave himself up to the vultures ! Or think of Scott's Journal, found among the snows, kept with faithful jealousy as long as the dying man had strength to hold a pen ! Let the imagination project itself into the minds of these three heroes—Livingstone in Africa, Burke in Australia, and Scott in Antarctica—and these records will straightway represent the stubborn revolt of noble minds against being incarcerated in a little period bounded by a birthday on the one side and a deathday on the other.   These journals reflect their stern and victorious determination to construct a bridge that should effectively connect them with generations postexistent to their own.

Ah, but the last word in bridge-building is not with the engineers.   The Church knows a wonderful secret.   She knows how to span yawning chasms in the presence of which the most daring architect would shudder and despair.   The Church exists to build bridges.   What are her peacemakers bu⸲

skilful engineers who know how to span the gulf
that yawns between lives that have become cruelly
divided ?   What are her prayer-meetings but bridges
of fearful and wonderful design ?

> There is a spot where spirits blend,
>   And friend holds fellowship with friend ;
> Though sundered far, by faith they meet
>   Around one common Mercy-seat.

What are her Communion Services but a triumphant defiance of all the separating tyrannies of
Time and Space ?   Around that table with the white
cloth the saints of all times and of all climes meet in
joyous brotherhood, and laugh to scorn the ages and
the oceans that can no longer separate.   What is
her deep note of warning but a paralysing horror of
a chasm that cannot be bridged ?   ' Between us and
you there is a great gulf *fixed*.'

What, indeed, is the Church's supreme message ?
It concerns a bridge, the most wonderful of all
bridges.   In his *Legend of the Eagles*, George d'Es-
partes says that the most heroic piece of self-sacrifice
known to history occurred in the building of a bridge
exactly a century ago.   ' It was in the depth of
winter, and the French Army, pressed on all sides
by the Cossacks, had to cross a river.   The enemy
had destroyed all the bridges, and Napoleon was

almost at his wits' end. Suddenly came the order that a bridge of some sort must be thrown across the river, and the men nearest the water, of course, were the first to carry out the almost impossible task. Several were swept away by the furious tide. Others, after a few minutes, sank through cold and exhaustion ; but more came, and the work proceeded as fast as possible. At last the bridge was completed, and the army reached the opposite bank in safety. Then followed a dramatic scene one of the most horrible recorded in the annals of any nation. When the men who had built the bridge were called out of the water, not one moved. Clinging to the pillars, there they stood silent and motionless. It was soon found that they had been frozen to death, their arms rigidly fixed against the woodwork in the attitude of Caryatides—the Caryatid of death. Napoleon, who witnessed the awful scene, could not, in spite of his impassive temperament, restrain his tears.'

Many bridges have been built by sacrifice. Cortes wept as he beheld his brave Spaniards fill with their writhing bodies the gaps in the Mexican causeway so that their comrades in the rear might march to safety over heaps of valiant dead. But what of these ? The world has seen a bridge that has moved the tears of men and of angels. The one magnificent ver ity of the Christian gospel is the stupendous fact that the chasm which yawned between man and God has been triumphantly spanned, and spanned from the divine side, and spanned so perfectly that the weakest and the wickedest can now cross where before the mightiest must have perished. The Cross is the most amazing achievement in the architecture of all God's wonderful worlds. All heaven felicitates the happy man who, unable to endure a yawning chasm of estrangement between his God and himself, sets out, by way of that bridge, to pass the dreadful gulf. There is nothing in the heavens above, nor on the earth beneath, to be compared with *that*.

III

THE DAINTIES IN THE DUNGEON

THE scene is laid in the villainous old prison at Marseilles. In one of its most loathsome and repulsive dungeons lay two men. For one of them, Monsieur Rigaud, a sumptuous meal had been provided. The other, John Baptist Cavalletto, had a hard, black crust. ' Rigaud soon dispatched his delicate viands,' Dickens tells us, ' and proceeded to suck his fingers as clean as he could. Then he paused in his drink to contemplate his fellow prisoner.

' How do you find the bread ? '

' A little dry, but I have my old sauce here,' returned John, holding up his knife.

' How sauce ? '

' I can cut my bread so—like a melon. Or so—like an omelette. Or so—like a fried fish. Or so—like a Lyons sausage,' said John, demonstrating the various cuts on the bread he held, and soberly chewing what he had in his mouth.

Now, I am not sure whether this should be called magic. It certainly is a kind of magic. The happy prisoner waves his hand over his crust and cries ' Presto ! ' ; and straightway it is transformed into melon, omelette, fried fish, or sausage at his will. I am not writing an article on criminology or prison management, but certainly the passage I have quoted from *Little Dorrit* could be made the text for such a screed.   It is a wicked waste of public money to support a man in a jail, when, by some wondrous witchery within him, he can transform his prison into a palace, and convert his frugal fare into fried fish.

A very wonderful witchery this.   By means of it Charles Lamb turned all the streets of London into pavements of pure gold.   ' I know,' the gentle Elia says, ' an alchemy that turns her mud into that precious metal.   I know ! '   Alchemy, witchery, magic—what is it ?   Yes, it is magic, I feel sure ; the most magical of all magic—what Richard Jefferies felicitously called ' wood magic.'   We remember the two boys, the pond a few yards across, and the raft made out of a packing-case.   Suddenly, by this wild and wondrous magic that transforms a dry crust into fried fish and sausage, the pond becomes the ' New Sea,' and they are explorers and adventurers.

' Let us go round it.   We have never been quite round it,' said Bevis.

' So we will,' said Mark ; ' but we shall not be
back to dinner.'

' As if travellers ever thought of dinner ! Of
course we shall take our provisions with us.'

' Let's go and get our spears,' said Mark.

' Oh, yes ; and the compass and the maps ; wait
a minute. We ought to have a medicine chest ;
the savages will worry us for physic ; and very
likely we shall have dreadful fevers.'

' Yes, and we must keep a diary,' said Mark,
' and when we go to sleep, who shall watch first,
you or I ? '

' Oh, we'll light a fire,' said Bevis, ' that will
frighten the lions ; they will glare at us, but they
can't stand fire. You hit them on the head with
a burning stick.'

Now, here we have a dirty puddle and a dusty
packing-case suddenly transformed, by what the
genial naturalist calls ' wood magic,' into an uncharted sea with desert islands, savage tribes, and
ferocious beasts. It is clearly the same species of
alchemy by which our poor prisoner at Marseilles
turned his dry crust into fried fish and sausage.
And I confess that, of the two, I scarcely know which
to admire the more. For if some superficial critic
remonstrates with me, and points out that with
Bevis and Mark the whole thing was a furious frolic,

whilst with the French prisoner it was a fine philosophy, I am bound to answer that it is by just such furious frolics that we have won the world. It is true that Bevis and Mark were only having a game ; but it is also true that your Columbuses and Cooks, your Tasmans and Dampiers, your Raleighs and Drakes, were all playing exactly the same game. It was because their fancy built up strange continents across the unsailed seas that they set out in search of the fairylands of which they dreamed. The triumphs of scientific discovery all follow the same law. When you have mastered the magic by which the crust became a fish, and by which the packing-case became a stately ship in full sail, you at once understand Newton's flight of fancy from a falling apple to a falling moon.

Here is a bargain ! If you will undertake to explain to me the process of alchemy or witchery by which the fried fish and sausage evolved from the hard black bread, and if you will tell me exactly how the gallant barque and the sea with a thousand shores evolved from the broken packing-case and the muddy pool, then, in return, I will undertake to tell you how this wonderful twentieth-century world of ours, with its wireless telegrams, its airships and its submarines, evolved from the Garden of Eden. I feel quite sure that Dickens himself felt that there was a connexion between the power by which poor Cavalletto turned a dry crust into appetizing dainties and the power by which a tiny world has been changed into a tremendous one. For Cavalletto, too, was an explorer in his way. He knew, not only how to find a fried fish in a dry crust, but how to find a broad continent in a narrow cell. Listen!

' What is the time ? ' asked Monsieur Rigaud.

' The mid-day bells will ring in forty minutes.'

' Why, you are a clock ; how is it that you always know ? '

' Oh, I always know what the hour is and where I am. I was brought in here at night, and out of a boat, but I know where I am. See here ! Marseilles harbour ' ; on his knees on the pavement, mapping it all out with a swarthy forefinger, ' Toulon (where the galleys are), Spain over there, Algiers over there. Creeping away to the left here, Nice. Round by the cornice to Genoa, Genoa Mole and harbour. Quarantine Ground. City there ; terrace gardens blushing with the belladonna. Here, Porto Fino. Stand out for Leghorn. Out again for Civita Vecchia. So away to—hey ! there's no room for Naples ' ; he had got to the wall by this time ; ' but it's all one ; it's in there ! ' Cavalletto could cruise round Europe without opening his cell door or looking out of its windows.

Now, coming back to the point at which I threatened to invade criminology, how on earth are you going to imprison a man whose witchery can turn crusts into delicacies, and who calmly takes into his cell with him half the face of Europe ?   There are some men who simply cannot be imprisoned ; and it is a waste of money to put them in jail.   They not only do not depend upon their environment, they decline to recognize their environment.   It simply does not swim into their ken.   And if you make their environment disagreeable, they will detach themselves from their environment, as a lizard detaches itself from its tail ; and will escape without it.

A couple of stories occur to me.   In the days of the Maori War some hostile natives resolved to insult Bishop Selwyn.   They arranged to offer him a pig-sty for his accommodation.   The Bishop accepted ;   drove out the pigs ;   gathered some fern from the bush for his bed ; and occupied his lowly residence with such charm and dignity that the Maories exclaimed : ' You cannot degrade that man ! '   Precisely !   He politely declined to identify himself with his environment.   The other story is from John Wesley's *Journal*.   John Nelson, one of Wesley's original helpers, was arrested and thrust into a horrible dungeon.   His record of the experience makes good reading : ' When I came into the dungeon, that stank worse than a hog-sty, by reason of the blood and filth that ran into it from the slaughter-house above, my soul was so filled with the love of God that it was a paradise to me ! ' Now, I ask again, what is the good of putting men like these into pig-sties and prisons ?

This is a wonderful thing—perhaps the most wonderful of all wonderful things.   It means that the world through which I move is simply a reflection of my own inmost self.   It is a mirror, as George Eliot said.   ' Laugh, and it laughs back ; frown, and your gloom is recast.'   If I have a princely soul, every prison or pig-sty that I enter flashes by this wondrous magic into a palace.   If I am a felon, I may live in a palace, but the palace will be as gloomy as a jail.   That is a tremendous saying of Maeterlinck's : ' Nothing befalls us that is not of the nature of *ourselves*.   Whether you climb up the mountain, or go down to the valley, none but *yourself* shall you meet on the highway of fate.   If Judas go forth to-night, it is towards Judas that his steps will tend, nor will chance for betrayal be lacking ; but let Socrates open his door, he shall find Socrates asleep on the threshold before him, and there will be occasion for wisdom.'   Wordsworth was once asked why he wrote of ' dancing daffodils.'   Daffodils do not

dance.   He reflected for a long time, and then replied that he could only suppose that, since the sight
of the daffodils set his soul dancing with delight, he
had unconsciously transferred the inward sensation
to the outward object.   Of course !

> It's a gay old world when you're gay,
>> And a glad world when you're glad ;
>>> But whether you play
>>> Or must toil all day,
> It's a sad old world when you're sad.

> It's a grand old world if you're great,
>> And a mean old world if you're small ;
>>> It's a world full of hate
>>> For the foolish who prate
> Of the uselessness of it all.

> It's a beautiful world to see,
>> Or it's dismal in every zone ;
>>> The thing it must be
>>> In its gloom or its glee
> Depends on yourself alone.

What could be more perfectly natural ?   It was
just because the prisoner at Marseilles had a soul
that was palatial that the jail became big enough to
hold half of Europe, and it was because everything
was delicate and dainty in his own heart that his
crust became transformed into delicacies and dainties.

You put a bishop into a pig-sty, and the pig-sty becomes an episcopal palace. You put a pig into a palace, and the palace becomes a sty.

Now, I repeat that it is a waste of public funds to imprison some men. What is the good of shutting Cavalletto up in your villainous jail, with a stone floor for his bed and a crust for his breakfast, if he is going to spend his time cruising about the coast of Europe, and feasting on melons, omelettes, fried fish, and sausage ? What is the good of flinging John Nelson into a foul dungeon if he is going to convert it into a perfect paradise ?   What is the use of putting John Bunyan into Bedford Jail if he is going to fill his cell with the Sisters from the Palace Beautiful, the Shepherds from the Delectable Mountains, and even the Palace and the Mountains themselves ?

We have all chuckled over the letter written by the puzzled Pliny to Trajan the Emperor concerning the Christians. The poor proconsul is at his wits' ends. He has found a class of criminals for whom his most horrible punishments and his most loathsome prisons have no terror. Indeed, they seem to like these things ; for the more he persecutes, the more ' the contagion of the superstition spreads ! ' The imprisoned Christians sing in their cells, and the dying martyrs greet the unseen with a cheer.

Prisons become palaces to them, and their hardest crusts are transformed into angels' food. Pliny confesses to his imperial master that he is perfectly bewildered. Again, when one of the early confessors appeared before the Roman Emperor, charged with being a Christian, the Emperor threatened him with banishment unless he renounced Christ. The Christian replied, ' Thou canst not, for the world is my Father's house.' ' But I will slay thee,' said the Emperor. ' Nay, but thou canst not, for my life is hid with Christ in God.' ' I will take away thy treasures.' ' Nay, but thou canst not,' was the reply, ' for my treasure is in heaven, and my heart is there.' ' But I will drive thee away from man, and thou shalt have no friend left.' ' Nay, but thou canst not,' once more said the confessor, ' for I have a Friend in heaven, from whom thou canst not separate me. I defy thee ; there is nothing thou canst do to hurt me.' What is the use of imprisoning men of this temper ? They escape, not *from* the prison, but *in* the prison. Like the three Hebrew children, they walk unharmed in the midst of the flame. When we were very young, we used to read fairy tales that told of magic cloaks that rendered their wearers invisible and invulnerable ; and we laughed at the fantastic notion. But we have learned since then of more wondrous witchery.

The Dainties in the Dungeon

There is a magic that turns prisons into palaces and crusts into dainties. There is a wonder that wraps a man about, and thenceforth no humiliation can degrade him, no banishment can exile him, no poverty can make him poor, and no death can destroy him.

IV

ETIQUETTE

THE old gardener at Versailles was in sad distress.
What pains he took with his flower-beds! How
patiently he mapped them all out in the evening,
and how deftly he executed his own designs in the
daytime! How he longed for the summer, that he
might feast his eyes upon the perfect patterns and
the beautifully blending blossoms! But that joy
was never his! For as soon as he had got his rare
seed nicely sown, his fragile plants fondly set, and
his delicate young cuttings tastefully arranged, the
courtiers from the palace trampled them all down,
and reduced the poor gardener to tears. Season
after season the noblemen and great ladies in their
strolls among the beautiful terraces and graceful
parterres, ruthlessly destroyed the cunning labour
of the old man's skilful hands. Till at last he could
endure it no longer. He would appeal to the king!
So right into the august presence of the great Louis
the Fourteenth the poor old gardener made his way,
and confided all his sorrows and disappointments

to his royal master.   And the king was sorry for the
old man, and ordered little tablets—' etiquette '—
to be neatly arranged along the sides of the flower-
beds, and a State order was issued commanding all
his courtiers to walk carefully within the etiquette.
And so the old gardener not only protected the
flowers that he loved from the pitiless feet of the
high-born vandals, but he enriched our vocabulary
with a new and startlingly significant word.

The art of life consists in keeping carefully within
the ways marked out by the etiquette.   From
cannibalism to culture is a long way.   And the
individual or the race that sets out on that pilgrimage forfeits more and more of freedom at every step.
The cannibal can do as he likes, and have what he
wants, and go where he pleases.   He tramples
without restraint on all life's flower-beds.   But as
he moves towards civilization he finds himself becoming subject to all sorts of rules and regulations.
' Thou shalt ' and ' Thou shalt not ' speak out
imperiously.   He must not do this, and he must not
have that ; he must not touch here, and he must not
go there.   His path is marked out by the etiquette.
And the more refined and cultured he becomes, the
more those laws subdivide and multiply.   He must
not only do this thing ; but he must do it in a certain
way.   He must not only go to this place, but he

must go at a certain time, and dressed in a certain fashion, and stay for just so long. Cannibalism is freedom—and wretchedness. Civilization is bondage—and delight.

For the beauty of it is that the pleasures of King Louis' lords and ladies were not at all curtailed, but were really very considerably increased, by the introduction of the etiquette. I can easily imagine that for a month or two, whilst they were chafing under the new restrictions, and whilst as yet the gardener's precious bulbs were but slowly developing towards their coming glory, the courtiers thought of the old man as a boor, a nuisance, and an enemy to their freedom. Why could they not tread wherever they liked? But afterwards, when their well-kept promenade was fringed and bordered by the most rare and beautiful and fragrant blossoms, then they blessed the old man as a benefactor, and laughed at their earlier folly. It is a very ancient heresy. Ever since the soul of the first man revolted against the etiquette that marked off one tree in the midst of the garden, the minds of men have rebelled against the royal legends, ' Thou shalt ' and ' Thou shalt not.' We abhor, as we saunter through the park, being eternally commanded to ' Keep off the grass.' We forget that it is only through the instrumentality of that obnoxious mandate that there is any grass left for us to keep off. The verdant and velvety lawn that charms the eye and soothes the sense is the triumph of the etiquette that sounds like tyranny. The truth is that I never enter into my best inheritance by putting my foot upon it. I more often come into my own by keeping my foot carefully off it. The world is too wisely arranged to play into the hands of the tramplers and the trespassers. The etiquette that subtracts from my freedom multiplies my felicity. Otherwise the cannibal and the criminal would be the happiest men breathing. Things never work out that way.

The courtiers learned in time that it is not necessary to trample upon a thing in order to enjoy it. We are most of us somewhat slow in making that discovery. In *The Roadmender* Michael Fairless tells us how she came upon a beautiful island out in the river, smothered with a riot of radiant flowers. ' At the upper end of the field,' she says, ' the river provides yet closer sanctuary for the daffodils. Held in its embracing arms lies an island, long and narrow, some thirty feet by twelve, a veritable untrod Eldorado, glorious in gold from end to end, just a fringe of weeds by the water's edge, and save for that—all daffodils. A great oak stands at the meadow's neck, an oak with gnarled and wandering roots, where one may rest, for it is bare of daffodils save for a group of three, and a solitary one apart growing close to the old tree's side.' Michael Fairless sat down beside the lonely little daffodil and feasted her eyes on the island in the stream. It was ' a sea of triumphant, golden heads, tossing blithely as the wind swept down to play with them at his pleasure.' And as she watched under the oak, and gazed upon the cloth of gold on the island, she exclaimed, ' It is *all mine* to have and to hold without severing a single slender stem or harbouring a thought of covetousness ; *mine*, as the whole earth is mine, to appropriate to myself without the burden and bane of worldly possession.'

Now here we have a very beautiful picture. Let us pause to reflect upon some of the questions that its beauty suggests. Why are there only four lonely little daffodils here by the gnarled old oak on the river's bank ? and why is this island out in the stream a tossing sea of gold ? The answer is obvious. The water round the island is like the tablets round the flower-beds. It is *liquid etiquette*. And, so far from impoverishing the strollers on the bank, it greatly enriches them. This girl sitting under the oak gazing on the golden glory of the island tells us that she felt, not like a courtier only, but like a queen. No palace on the planet held a princess so conscious of her wondrous wealth as was she in that delicious hour.   It was just because she could not set foot upon her inheritance that it was so splendidly and delightfully her own.

But perhaps the best illustration would have been the case of Richard Jefferies.   Everybody who has read Mr. Edward Thomas's beautiful life of the young English naturalist knows how, in his brave fight with a cruel disease and with grinding poverty, Jefferies was comforted every day by the sight of the wild life around him and the sense of its complete and glorious possession.   It was all his ; and it was his just because he never tried to touch or tame it.   Hear what he says : ' Every blade of grass was *mine*,' he cries exultingly, ' as if I had myself planted it.   All the grasses were my pets : I loved them all. Perhaps that was why I never had a pet, never cultivated a flower, never kept a caged bird.   Why keep pets when every wild hawk that passed over my head was *mine* ?   I joyed in his swift, careless flight, in the throw of his pinions, in his rush over the elms and miles of woodland.   What more beautiful than the sweep and curve of his going through the azure sky ?   I see the lark chase his mate over the low stone wall of the ploughed field, to battle with his high-crested rival, to balance himself on his trembling wings, outspread a few yards above the earth, and utter that sweet little loving kiss, as it

were, of song. Oh, happy, happy days ! So beautiful to watch ; and all *mine* ! ' It was just because
the poor, frail young naturalist kept his feet off the
flower-beds, never caged a bird or potted a plant,
that all the birds of the forest, and the flowers of
the field, seemed so thoroughly and gloriously his
own.

Life is all a matter of etiquette. Louis the
Fourteenth never supposed for a moment that the
dainty little tablets would prevent the courtiers
from trampling on the bulbs if they were determined to do so. The tablets indicate the king's
pleasure, that is all. Indeed, that is all that
etiquette ever does. It is indicative, not imperative.
God does not protect His flower-beds with impregnable fortresses. He makes the way perfectly clear
to a man ; but if the man has set his heart on outraging the etiquette, there is nothing to prevent him.
God in His mercy *hedges* our way about with His
commandments, His exhortations, His revelations ;
but it is the easiest thing in the world to break
through a *hedge*. Bunyan's pilgrims made that
discovery.

' The way was rough, and their feet tender ; so
the souls of the pilgrims were much discouraged
because of the way. So they went to the fence, and
saw soft grass in the meadow on the other side.

' " Come, good Hopeful," said Christian, " and let us get over."

' " But how," replied the suspicious Hopeful, " how if this should lead us out of the way ? "

' " That's not like," said Christian.

' So Hopeful, being persuaded by his fellow, went after him over the stile.'

But the story does not end there. On the soft green grass beyond the fence the pilgrims were captured by Giant Despair, and flung into the dark dungeons of Doubting Castle. And, half a dozen pages further on, Bunyan tells how, sadder and wiser men, after their escape, they climbed back over the fence on to the road they had formerly left.

' And when they were gone over the stile, they began to contrive what they should do to prevent other pilgrims from falling into the hands of Giant Despair. So they erected a pillar, and engraved upon the side thereof this sentence : " Over this stile is the way to Doubting Castle, which is kept by Giant Despair, who despiseth the King of the Celestial Country, and seeketh to destroy His holy pilgrims." Many, therefore, that followed after, read what was written, and escaped the danger.' It is perfectly plain to me that Bunyan's fence, and Michael Fairless's river round the island, and King Louis the Fourteenth's tablets round the flower

beds, and even the pillar erected by the pilgrims
beside the treacherous stile, are all different ways of
saying the same thing.   It is all a matter of etiquette.

Now, this illustration from *Pilgrim's Progress*
reminds me.   Whilst I was perfectly right in saying
just now that God does not protect His flower-beds
with frowning forts, I was perfectly wrong if I gave
the impression that trespassers will not be prosecuted.
The pilgrims quickly discovered that severe penalties
lurked in wait for them on the other side of the
fence.   There is a quaint old text that expresses the
truth of this matter about as nicely as it can be
stated. ' *Whoso breaketh a hedge,*' said a very wise
man once, perhaps not without a wince, as memory
reminded him of his own hedge-breaking, ' *whoso
breaketh a hedge, a serpent shall bite him.*'   I confess
that I never quite understood what this very wise
man meant by the serpent until I sat at the feet of
a very wise woman.   And the very wise woman
made plain what the very wise man had left obscure.
' Would you judge of the lawfulness or unlawfulness
of pleasure ? ' good Susanna Wesley asked of her
son John. ' Then,' she added, ' take this rule.
Whatever weakens your reason, impairs the tenderness of your conscience, obscures your sense of God,
or takes off the relish of spiritual things, *that* is
sin to you.'   Sin is, of course, the outraging of

etiquette. And here, according to Susanna Wesley, one of the world's very greatest and very wisest, and very saintliest women, here are the bites of the serpents : ' The weakening of the reason, the impaired tenderness of the conscience, the obscured sense of God, the lost relish for the spiritual.'

And when this wise and holy woman—the mother of the Wesleys—talks in this strain, she frightens me. She describes these symptoms with such skill that I feel the horrid virus in my own veins. I have outraged the divine etiquette myself. I have trampled on the King's flower-beds ; I have clambered over the stile like Bunyan's pilgrims ; I have broken through the hedge, and the snake has bitten me. I am glad that Moses lifted up the serpent in the wilderness, and I am thankful that the Saviour left us in no doubt as to the meaning of that weird and wondrous symbol. All the etiquette of the law is designed to keep a man from trampling on the flowers : and all the etiquette of the gospel marks out for contrite trespassers the way that leads up to the Cross.

V

CHRYSANTHEMUMS

IT is very wonderful, the way in which the most discordant and incongruous experiences of life mix themselves together in our dreams.   I had been to a chrysanthemum show.   I am not particularly fond of shows.   Very few things are at their best when on exhibition, and even flowers look somehow excited and tumbled at these unnatural displays.   The chrysanthemums did not seem quite themselves in the stuffy atmosphere of the crowded hall.   Still, chrysanthemums are chrysanthemums ; and even chrysanthemums on show are very lovely things. There is a certain flaunting abandon about chrysanthemums that one does not notice in other flowers. These waving tassels of white and purple and gold are very attractive, and the penetrating perfume is almost overpowering.   And yet, with all their bravery, there is a certain indescribable sadness about these gorgeous blossoms.   They are autumn visitants.   And they seem to whisper of a glory that lingers about our path, even when all seems to

be rushing to decay. ' The narcissus, the rose, and
the chrysanthemum-—these,' writes Mr. C. E. Shea,
' are the natural emblems of our human life ! Bright
youth, with all before us, and no cloud to dim the sky
—the narcissus. Maturity and power—the rose.
And then, through the more sober and perhaps
sadder period of later life, when sometimes a strong
faith is needed to make us realize that the gathering
clouds have still a silver lining, and that there remains behind them a sun which may yet shine for us
—our floral help and cultivator, the chrysanthemum.'

I went home from the show. I sat for a moment
or two before the fire, with my Bible for company.
I sat captivated by those great words of Paul to the
Philippians : ' Be careful for nothing . . . and the
peace of God, which passeth all understanding, shall
guard your hearts and minds in Christ Jesus.' I
fear I must have dozed. For, all at once, I saw a
garden. The bed was overgrown with weeds. Beside it stood the Master and the gardener. In His
hand the Master held three rare and radiant chrysanthemums. They formed a perfect riot of floral
glory. Their flowing petals were like fluttering
tassels of beauty. Their fragrance was delicious.
' Grow chrysanthemums like these,' said the Master
to the gardener, ' and I will bring you the seed
of the sweetest Heart's-ease with which to make

a border round the bed.' The gardener eyed the exquisite blossoms admiringly, and then, close to the Master's fingers, he caught sight of a tiny label with which the wind was playfully toying. He straightway examined it. The gay chrysanthemums were labelled CHEERFULNESS—' Be careful for nothing.' And then a look of wonderful insight and understanding overspread the countenance of the gardener. ' Yes,' repeated the Master deliberately, ' if you can grow chrysanthemums like these in the bed here, I will give you the rarest Heart's-ease for a border— " the peace of God which passeth all understanding." ' The Master moved silently away, and left the gardener looking at the bed.

But, oh, it is one thing to talk about beautiful flowers, and it is another thing to grow them. For just look at the weeds ! Rudyard Kipling was right when he sang :

Our England is a garden, and such gardens are not made
By singing ' *Oh, how beautiful* ! ' and sitting in the shade,
While better men than we go out and start their working
    lives,
At grubbing weeds from gravel-paths with broken dinner-
    knives.

Now, I happen to know quite intimately the gardener who tries to grow these glorious blossoms.

And I know that *that* is precisely his difficulty. It is every gardener's difficulty. ' I have just turned gardener,' says Lord Macaulay, in one of his charming letters to his sister ; ' I have just been putting creepers round my window, forming beds of rhododendrons round my fountain. I have had no friends near me, and no enemies but *those execrable dandelions* ! ' Ah ! those dandelions ! Writing to his little niece, he says again : ' I thought that I was rid of the villains ; but the day before yesterday, when I got up and looked out of my window, I could see five or six of their great, flaring, yellow faces turned up at me. " Only you wait till I come down ! " I cried. How I grubbed them up ! How I enjoyed their destruction ! Is it Christian-like to hate a dandelion so savagely ? ' That is precisely the trouble about gardening. It is not all poetry. It is largely perspiration. ' All the old sadness is piled up in a garden,' said the kindly Piper in Myrtle Reed's *Spinner in the Sun,* ' and there are weeds in every life.' Exactly. I used to think that if I would have the Master's Heart's-ease—the peace that passeth all understanding—I had but to ask for it. I have learned since that the Master is wiser than that. He knows that the dandelions would smother it. And therefore He bids me cultivate chrysanthemums, for he knows that, by the time that these fair flowers are flourishing, the dandelions will all be dead.

Yes, He bids me grow chrysanthemums. Now, it is the glory of the chrysanthemum that it seems to defy its frigid and chilling surroundings. It flourishes amidst the frosts. Its brilliant petals are like waving tongues of flame blazing a grand and triumphant defiance to the wintry atmosphere which enfolds them. It is in its glory when all other flowers are dead. ' Be careful for nothing,' it seems to say. Be the conqueror, and not the slave, of your environment. No character in fiction has charmed us more than brave Mark Tapley. We have all fallen in love with him. He was for ever and for ever growing chrysanthemums. He saw no credit in being jolly when everything went well ; but when others were ' sae weary full o' care ' he was ' careful for nothing.' His heart sang amidst the dreariest gloom. And even when disaster reached its climax in the pestilential American swamp, and when poor Martin Chuzzlewit's heart was breaking with the cruelty and the chagrin of it all, then Mark was at his brightest and his best. Says Dickens : ' When the log-hut had received them, Martin lay down on the ground and wept aloud. " Lord love you, sir," cried Mr. Tapley in great terror ; " don't do that, don't do that, anything but that ; it never helped man, woman, or child over the lowest fence yet, and it never will ; anything but that. . . . Here we are . . . everything in its proper place, here's the salt pork, here's the biscuit, here's the tin pot—this tin pot is a small fortune in itself—here's the blankets, here's the axe ; who says we ain't got a first-rate set-out ? I feel as if I was a cadet gone out to Indy, and my father was Chairman of the Board of Directors ; here we are, sir, all complete. For what we are going to receive—Lord bless you, sir, it's very like a gipsy party." ' Mark Tapley was growing his chrysanthemums.

And chrysanthemums are worth growing, as Paul knew very well. I need not have come down to modern fiction for my illustration, after all. This very letter to the Philippians is as fine a chrysanthe-mum as I could desire. What a letter it is ! It seems set to music. It is written in a wretched cell by an old man of tottering health, whose hopes are all shattered, whose plans are all thwarted, whose prospects are all in ruin and decay. Yet it fairly ripples with sacred mirth, and sings out bravely the gaiety of its writer's heart. ' Rejoice,' the old prisoner cries, ' rejoice in the Lord alway, and again I say, " Rejoice ! " ' It is like the blithe song of a nightingale in a darksome English lane. It is melody breaking out of misery. It is gaiety conquering

gloom. ' Be full of care about nothing,' Paul says ;
and we see, as he says it, that he has himself learned
his lesson well. His flowers are flourishing amidst the
frosts. One who can grow chrysanthemums to such
perfection is entitled to urge their culture upon others.

Some people have a perfect genius for growing
chrysanthemums. There is on record a conversation between Daniel Webster and some of his
illustrious compeers. Somebody raised the question
as to which was the finest passage in the Bible.
One argued for the Creation story, another for the
Sermon on the Mount, and a third for the description
of the redeemed in the book of Revelation. But
Webster slowly quoted those exquisite verses from
one of the minor prophets : ' Although the fig-tree
shall not blossom, neither shall fruit be in the vines ;
the labour of the olive shall fail, and the fields shall
yield no meat ; the flock shall be cut off from the
fold, and there shall be no herd in the stalls : yet
I will rejoice in the Lord, I will joy in the God of my
salvation.' ' I am amazed,' said Webster, ' that
no talented artist has seen there a subject for a
masterpiece—the prophet Habakkuk sitting in the
midst of his dreadful desolation, still praising God
and rejoicing in his unseen Saviour ! ' Habakkuk
was ' careful for nothing '—he was growing chrysanthemums.

I think of Job singing amidst his maze of sorrow
and mystery of pain : ' Though He slay me, yet
will I trust in Him.'   There was a chrysanthemum
for you !   I think of Uncle Tom shouting his jubilant
camp-meeting choruses whilst the blood drawn by
the slave-whip trickles down his back.   I think of
the Salvationist sister smiling her way, day after
day, amidst the suffocating smells, the strident
sounds, and the disgusting sights of a squalid
London slum.   I think of the missionary at his lonely
outpost bravely maintaining his gracious witness
amidst the apparently impregnable strongholds of
superstition.   I think of a bed-ridden sufferer whom
it is my privilege to visit, and whose face is always
radiant with a glory that hides the furrows ploughed
by pain.   I think of an old pilgrim of my acquaintance.   His hair reminds you of the winter snows ;
but the joy of his heart, as it escapes through his
eyes, recalls the glorious blossoms that flourish
amidst the frosts.   ' The outward man perishes,'
he says, ' but the inward man is renewed day by
day.'   These folk all know how to grow chrysanthemums.

But a story leaps to my mind that leads me higher
still, and seems to leave both Dickens and Paul a long
way behind.   F. W. Robertson one day preached
a great sermon on the insistence and sacredness of

common duty. He seemed like a prophet of fire as he called on the people to do something worth while. A lady came to him in the vestry afterwards. 'Such preaching will get you into trouble, Mr. Robertson!' she said. 'I don't care!' exclaimed the fervid and excited preacher. 'Mr. Robertson,' the lady expostulated, 'do you know where "Don't care" came to?' 'Yes,' answered Robertson, '"Don't care" came to *the Cross!*' That was finely spoken. There was a divine carelessness about Jesus. He was careful for nothing. There were chrysanthemums growing on the hill called Calvary.

'Grow chrysanthemums,' said the Master to the gardener, 'and I will give you Heart's-ease for a border round the bed. The peace of God that passeth all understanding shall guard your hearts and minds in Christ Jesus.' And the Master always keeps His word—always! I think at this moment of a pair of witnesses whom I could summon to prove it. After his splendid and triumphant warfare against slavery, William Wilberforce lay dying. His Quaker friend, J. J. Gurney, went to see him. The aged warrior was very frail and very feeble. He was swathed in flannels, and at the point of death. 'But,' says Gurney, 'he unfolded his own experience to me in a highly interesting manner. He told me that the text on which he was then most prone to dwell, and from which he was deriving peculiar comfort, was this: " Be careful for nothing ; . . . and the peace of God which passeth all understanding shall keep your hearts and minds through Christ Jesus." While his frail nature was at the point of collapse, and his mortal tabernacle seemed ready to be dissolved, this peace was his blessed and abundant portion.'

Now, it so happened that, at just about the same time, the saintly Charles Simeon was also passing to his reward, and his friend J. M. Neale gives us an account of a very similar experience with the very self-same text, at the bedside of the dying Simeon. What does this coincidence mean? Is it mere chance ? It is nothing of the kind. Read the context in both cases. See to what perfection these two devout and fervid souls had developed the grace of Cheerfulness ! What masters they both were in the high art of growing chrysanthemums ! They had become ' careful for nothing,' and therefore the peace of God which passeth all understanding was given with a royal hand. When we have torn out our dandelions, and have cultivated our chrysanthemums, the Master never forgets His promise, but rewards His patient gardeners with Heart's-ease in abundance.

VI

THE BRANCH ON THE BREAKERS

THAT was a great moment in the history of this little world. We all remember vividly the drawn-out agony of those dreadful days, and still more dreadful nights, through which Columbus held his way across the unknown western seas. All on board believed the land of their search to be a wild freak of their commander's disordered fancy.

> They sailed and sailed, as winds might blow,
>   Until at last the blanched mate said :
> ' Why, now not even God would know
>   Should I and all my men fall dead.
> These very winds forget their way,
>   For God from these dread seas is gone.
> Now speak, brave admiral, speak and say——'
>   He said : ' Sail on ! Sail on ! and on ! '

Two long months at sea ! They believed that they had sailed beyond the reach of man and beyond the care of God. They made Columbus promise that, unless in three more days they sighted land, he would turn his prow once more to the east. And then, on that third day, they saw, circling round the masts, *a land-bird,* and, tossing on the waves, *a branch with berries on it* !

Those who have travelled know something of the sensation.   I remember once spending nearly three weeks at sea without sighting so much as a sail. We knew that we were approaching Cape Horn. And, on a memorable Sunday morning, bitterly cold, but brilliantly sunny, a pure white pigeon made its appearance, and flew about the ship. It is a funny thing to look back upon ; the rails all round the decks black with hundreds of men and women, clambering and craning and straining, their faces flushed with excitement, all of them hungry to feast their eyes on this first harbinger of land : ' a land-bird and a branch with berries on it.'

Who can forget the pathos of that scene, in *Uncle Tom's Cabin,* when poor Eliza was escaping with her child from slavery ?   The bloodhounds were on her track.   She must make all the pace she can, yet the toddling feet of her babe were terribly tired.   But with womanly foresight ' she had provided in her little bundle a store of cakes and apples, which she used as expedients for quickening the speed of the child, rolling the apple some yards before him, when the boy would run with all his might after it ; and this ruse, often repeated, carried them over many a half-mile.' Wise negro woman ! Her cakes and apples were like the land-bird and the berries ; they lured the traveller on. They remind us of a quaint old Grecian legend. One there was, or so the story goes, who, cherishing an ardent affection for the young, secreted himself in ambush on the road that led to the temple. Whenever he saw a tired child loiter on the sacred path, he would roll a golden ball in front of the halting youth, and, making him forget his fatigue, set his feet hastening once more towards the solemn fane.

Now, life is full of such things as the cakes and apples from Eliza's basket, as the golden ball on the road to the temple ; full, that is to say, of things that egg us on ; full of land-birds and of branches with berries on them. One can easily imagine how the passionate enthusiasm of Columbus, which had led him to tramp across Europe begging for ships, and which had died down, like a fire burning itself out, during those long and fruitless weeks at sea, blazed grandly up again when the land-bird lighted on the rigging, and the berries tossed temptingly upon the waves. And exactly the same beautiful and cheering experience occasionally greets us all. I saw some boys engaging

in a paper-chase. They were the hounds, and they
had lost the scent of the hares. They had come a
long way, and were exhausted. After a perfunctory
search for the lost trail, they gave it up, and resolved
to go home along the road. But just at that
moment a straggler of the pack caught sight of a
fluttering tassel of paper on the hillside, and, with a
shout and a bound, they were off again in hot pursuit. It was ' a land-bird and a branch with berries
on it.' How frequently have we trudged along the
dusty and interminable road until, footsore and
dispirited, we have paused and leaned for a moment
upon a milestone or a stile! Was it really worth
while going on? Had we not better turn back?
And, even as we halted, we have caught sight, away
on the slopes of a distant hill, of the first twinkling
lights of the city that we sought. It was like ' a
land-bird and a branch with berries on it.' We
forgot our weariness, and forgave the long, long
road behind. It was immediately after the pilgrims
had been depressed and discouraged by their painful
imprisonment in Doubting Castle that they saw,
from the heights of the Delectable Mountains, the
glory of the Celestial City. That first clear vision
lured them on. It was ' a land-bird and a branch
with berries on it.'

I have just been reading Mr. Campbell N. Moody's

Saints in Formosa. Mr. Moody has a most interesting and suggestive chapter on ' Loiterers.' He
shows how an idolater will come for treatment to the
mission hospital, or stand, it may be, time after
time, listening to the voice of the preacher. Nothing
comes of it. The patient returns to his country
home, and resumes his idolatry, as though nothing
had happened. The casual hearer goes on his way,
and seems to have received no very deep impression.
But Mr. Moody shows that things are not what they
seem. He gives some very striking cases which
prove that away in his country home, and even
at his degrading altars, the patient is haunted
through the years by the memory of the teaching he
received at the hospital. And, many years afterwards, a very small incident—the arrival of another
preacher, or a chance meeting with a Chinese convert, or even the sight of a Christian church building
—will bring the earlier impression to actual fruition,
and lead the loiterer into the light of the gospel.
That small incident, precipitating a crisis, is ' a
land-bird and a branch with berries on it.'

What does all our preaching and teaching amount
to but to pointing out to disheartened mariners
' a land-bird and a branch with berries on it ' ? All
our definitions, and explanations, and expositions,
and Christian evidences, they are but crepuscular

intimations after all.   We never actually point out the land.   Dr. J. H. Jowett, of New York, put it very finely the other day.   ' Some minister of the Cross,' he said, ' toiling in great loneliness, among a scattered and primitive people, and on the very fringe of dark primaeval forests, sent me a little sample of his vast and wealthy environment.   It was a bright and gaily coloured wing of a native bird. The colour and life of trackless leagues sampled within the confines of an envelope !   And, when we have made a compact little phrase to enshrine the secret of Grace, I feel that, however fair and radiant it may be, we have only got a wing of a native bird, and bewildering stretches of wealth are untouched and unrevealed.   No, we cannot define it.' We have seen but ' a land-bird and a branch with berries on it.'

Or look along another line.   Missionaries laboured in Tahiti for twenty years without making a single convert.   They must have felt as Columbus felt after two months at sea.   Indeed, the directors of the mission actually met to consider the expediency of abandoning the station.   The missionaries were temporarily withdrawn in order to give their advice personally in London.   It was decided to make one more attempt.   The missionaries returned, and on their arrival in Tahiti made an astounding discovery.   The natives who had been their servants at the mission station in the earlier days had not only confessed the Saviour, but had met together regularly, in the absence of the missionaries, to implore the divine favour on the work of the mission. Here was ' a land-bird and a branch with berries on it ' !   The discouraged workers renewed their toil with radiant faces, with what amazing result the world very well knows.

The case of the Lone Star Mission is very similar. For thirty-six years Mr. Day and his helpers had laboured there in Southern India with little or no result.   At the American Baptist Annual Meetings in 1853, the delegates had to determine as to whether the work should be continued or abandoned.   In that crisis a light broke upon the soul of an eminent hymn-writer, Dr. S. F. Smith, the author of ' My Country, 'tis of thee.'   He heard the debate, and was filled with concern.   He returned to his lodgings, and penned the familiar lines beginning :

> Shine on, lone star !   Thy radiance bright
>   Shall spread o'er all the eastern sky ;
> Morn breaks apace from gloom and night,
>   Shine on, and bless the pilgrim's eye !

Next morning he read the poem to the Assembly. The effect was electric.   It was resolved to continue the work, and the church that resulted enfolded thousands of converts within its membership. Dr. Smith's inspiration was ' a land-bird and a branch with berries on it.'

I know a Sunday-school teacher. She had taken her class with conscientious regularity and admirable fidelity for years. But nothing came of it. She handed her resignation to the superintendent. As she left the building after doing so, one of her boys stopped her. Would she mind telling him just what it meant to join the Church? She went back and asked the superintendent for her letter. She tore it up unopened. She had seen ' a land-bird and a branch with berries on it.'

I say again that the experience is a very common one. It comes to us, for example, whenever we kneel to pray. God is so great ; heaven is so high ; how may I know that my heartbroken cry shall be heard of Him? ' Be comforted,' says Pascal ; ' thou wouldst not be seeking Him if thou hadst not already found Him ! ' The very inclination and desire to pray are from Him. They represent ' a land-bird and a branch with berries on it.'

Two great and beautiful scriptures occur to me as I lay down my pen. ' Ye were sealed with the Holy Spirit, that Spirit being a pledge and foretaste —an earnest—of our inheritance in anticipation of its full redemption.' And this : ' They had not received the promised blessings, but had seen them from a distance, and had greeted them, and had acknowledged themselves to be foreigners and strangers.' The New Testament writers combine to assure us that all that we have received of grace and mercy and spiritual favour is but a foretaste and a pledge of the good land before us. It is ' a land-bird and a branch with berries on it.' ' The patriarchs,' says Delitzsch, ' greeted the fulfilment of the promises from afar, as the wanderer greets his home, even when he only catches a glimpse of it in the distance.' We are reminded of Cowper's

> . . . . . . savage rock,
> That hides the sea-mew in its hollow clefts
> Above the reach of man. Its hoary head,
> Conspicuous many a league, the mariner,
> Bound homeward, and in hope already there,
> Greets with three cheers exulting.

Courage, then ! The country of our quest is not so doubtful as we think. The air is flecked with the snowy pinions of the land-birds, and the waves are strewn with branches having berries on them.

VII

THE BABY

A BABY spoils one for everything else. A baby is so delicious, so mysterious, so exquisite, that everything else seems horribly commonplace after the baby. There is simply nothing, either in the world or out of it, that can hold a candle to a real live baby. Carlyle never had any children. That explains a great deal. But I like to think of the stern old sage, in that last year of his life, nursing his cousin's baby. It opened a new world to the great man. Lecky tells us that he used to look down into its dimpled face with inexpressible amazement. He regarded it as a wonder of Nature. He used to speak of it as 'our baby,' and said that it was 'an odd kind of article,' and that it was 'very strange that Shakespeare should once have been like that!' I have a notion of my own that Shakespeare was Shakespeare just because he was once like that, and just because he kept the child-heart always with him. I have somewhere read of Kingsley that, being unutterably bored on one occasion by the solemnities and formalities of some public or social function, he at last broke from the terrible restraint. Throwing off his coat, he astounded every one present by challenging them to race him to the top branch of a giant tree near by. And in a few minutes half the company were scrambling like monkeys among the swinging boughs. That is just the sort of man to write *Westward Ho!* Could Dickens have taken his place in literature if he had lost the ripple of childish merriment from that wonderful soul of his? No, no, no; in literature, as in life, it is the *little child* that leads us. That is what the *prophet* said.

Poor little baby! Who can help pitying him? He seems so very much the sport of destiny, the child of fate. Was it altogether kind to involve him in all the amazing mysteries and endless problems of the universe without consulting him? Here he is, poor, sprawling, helpless little thing. Nobody asked him whether he wished to come. ' Our spoonful of existence is served out to us,' as a brilliant English essayist has put it, ' and no questions asked as to how we like it. Such points as to whether we would wake up in the twentieth century or in the old Stone period ; in Mars or on this planet ; whether we should be male or female ; prince, poet, or wood-cutter ; and a thousand other things deemed by us important—all were determined without the smallest reference to the opinions of that speck of vitality inside us which we call " ourselves." ' Mr. G. K. Chesterton, in *Heretics*, states the same peculiarity another way. ' The best way,' he says, ' in which a man could test his readiness to encounter the common variety of mankind would be to climb down a chimney into any house at random, and get on as well as possible with the people inside. And that is essentially what each one of us did on the day that he was born.' There is something very impressive about this shaping of a baby's destiny without consulting him. On a thousand small matters he will afterwards have his say. He may go this way or that way, do this thing or that thing. But the biggest issues of all he finds decided for him when he opens his eye upon them for the first time. Clearly, ' we are not our own.' That is what the *apostle* said.

A baby is a born leader. What a day that is in a woman's life when, pressing her very own baby to her breast, she feels the exquisite rapture of motherhood ! What a day that is in a man's life when he takes into his arms for the first time the dear child of his own body ! What happens on that day ? The little child leads them out into a larger, ampler, richer, more glorious life ; that is all. ' A little child shall lead them.' Our babies remain babies for so long, as compared with the furry babies of the fields and of the forests, because we need their leadership. Our hearts need to be softened, and our souls sweetened, by their gentle ministries, and so they do not hurry to grow up. And every day of their baby lives they beckon us on towards goodness. Michael Fairless, in *The Roadmender*, tells a lovely story of the grimy little waif who put up his lips to be kissed by the hardened and vicious old organ-grinder Gawdine. Gawdine shook him off with a blow and a curse. The little child scampered tearfully away. A day or two later Gawdine met with an accident. In the hospital he was haunted by the memory of the wistful and upturned face. When he left the wards, he set out to search for it. He had the jigs and tunes that children love put in his organ. He played in alleys and by-ways where children congregated. He never found the child of the upturned face. But, in searching, he became gentle and kind and serious and noble. Michael Fairless says that if she had to write his epitaph it would be : ' He saw the face of a little child, and looked on God.' Dickens tells in *The Old Curiosity Shop* of the little child who led the old man away from his gambling haunts to the pure life of the countryside, where he forgot his vices.

George Eliot tells of the little child who took the withered hand of the miser, taught him to make daisy chains, and led him into a love that was pure and unselfish and uplifting. ' A little child shall lead them.'

Now, the world is always wofully slow in recognizing the things that matter. Thackeray used to greatly amuse Macaulay by telling him of an incident which he actually witnessed at the London Zoo. A crowd had gathered around the enclosure in which the hippopotamus was confined. On one outskirt of the crowd stood Thackeray ; on another stood Macaulay. Macaulay's *History* had just been published, and was the talk of the town. Two young ladies in the throng were admiring the hippopotamus when some one drew their attention to the presence of the historian. ' Mr. Macaulay ! ' cried the lovely pair. ' Is that Mr. Macaulay ? Never mind the hippopotamus ! ' Precisely, it was the historian who was best worth looking at. Nobody knows now what became of the hippopotamus. The huge and ugly creature only emerges upon the history of the world through his chance association with that one incident. But Macaulay is immortal. Who would stare at a hippopotamus if he had the chance of seeing and hearing Macaulay ? Yet the unseeing crowd at the Zoo went on admiring the thick-skinned amphibian, and only two elect souls left the crowd to gaze upon Macaulay! That is the way of the world. It never sees the things best worth seeing. Take the newspaper for example. People tear open their newspapers to read of the wars and the accidents and the politics and the sports and the prosecutions, as though *these* were the things of most importance! The really sensational item in the newspaper is always to be found in the column headed Births, Marriages, and Deaths. Not among the deaths, for those chapters have closed. Nor among the marriages, for here the great choice has been made, and life has taken its shape and colour. But among *the births*! These babies! What startling and sensational and epoch-making items of news *these* announcements may represent! The cablegrams are mere hippopotami; Macaulay is *here*! 'A new universe is created,' Jean Paul Richter used to say, and to say truly, 'every time a child is born.' This is the way in which God cleanses and sweetens and brightens His world; and He has no other way of doing it. He has no other way, because He wants no other way. The baby is sufficient for the task. What a baby cannot do, cannot be done.

Yet who looks to the baby? Who turns to the baby as the strategic point in the struggle of nations?

It is always so ; we are for ever staring at the hippopotamus. Europe was never darker than when
Wyclif was born. But which of those villagers
in the little Yorkshire hamlet suspected, as he
saw that tiny baby in that modest cradle, that, with
his nativity, the new day had dawned ? Slavery
was most strongly entrenched when Abraham
Lincoln was born. Who that watched his baby
antics on the one hand, and listened to the cry of
the oppressed on the other, dreamed that the baby
before them was the key to the whole situation ?
No ; we never find room for the baby. He is
always in the manger. It never occurs to us, as we
confuse our minds with the world's worries and the
world's woes, that the baby in its swaddling-clothes
is really the way out. A century ago, for example,
men were following, with bated breath, the march
of Napoleon, and waiting with feverish impatience
for the latest news of the wars. And all the while,
in their own homes, babies were being born. But
who could think about *babies* ? Everybody was
thinking about *battles*. It was another case of the
historian and the hippopotamus. For let us look
at some of those babies. Why, in one year, lying
midway between Trafalgar and Waterloo, there
stole into the world a host of heroes ! During that
one year, 1809, Mr. Gladstone was born at Liverpool ;

Alfred Tennyson was born at the Somersby rectory ; and Oliver Wendell Holmes made his first appearance at Massachusetts. On the very self-same day of that self-same year Charles Darwin made his début at Shrewsbury, and Abraham Lincoln drew his first breath at Old Kentucky. Music was enriched by the advent of Frederic Chopin at Warsaw, and of Felix Mendelssohn at Hamburg. Within the same year, too, Samuel Morley was born at Homerton, Edward FitzGerald at Woodbridge, Elizabeth Barrett Browning at Durham, and Frances Kemble in London. But nobody thought of babies. Everybody was thinking of battles. Yet, viewing that age in the truer perspective which the distance of a hundred years enables us to command, we may well ask ourselves which of the battles of 1809 mattered more than the babies of 1809 ?

During the next few years, whilst Wellington and Soult were still struggling in the Peninsular War, Thackeray, and Dickens, and Bright, and Browning, and Livingstone, and a hundred other historic babies were born. But who cared ? Who, for example took any notice of that baby at Blantyre ? Children, feeling the first faint hint of spring in the air, paused to play for awhile on the green, and then scampered home to tell their mothers that there was a new baby down at Neil Livingstone's store.

But the excitement ended there.   It was no time for gossip about babies.   Down at the corner, where the crazy fingerpost marked the spot where the village lane joined the long main road, knots of eager men waited impatiently for the lumbering old stage-coach to bring news from the war.   Europe was getting ready for Waterloo.   And in Neil Living-stone's odorous store, through those long evenings, half a dozen sturdy Scotsmen gathered to discuss the latest intelligence that had filtered through to Blantyre.   What would Napoleon do next?   Could he raise another army now that the stupend-ous proportions of the Moscow disaster had been realized?   How fared the great Duke in the Penin-sula?   These were the questions that those brawny northerners discussed as they squatted on empty cases or leaned against the counter.   For had not Neil Livingstone two brothers with Wellington at the front?   And of what consequence, in comparison, was the puny baby whose shrill scream occasionally punctuated the conversation?   How squalidly mi-croscopic that baby seemed!   And yet whilst they discussed countries that baby represented a con-tinent, a continent as big as Europe and India and China and Australia put together!   The key of a new world was locked up in his heart.   The baby was David Livingstone.   That is always the blunder we short-sighted people make. We fancy that God can only manage His world by big battalions abroad, when all the while He is doing it by beautiful babies at home. When a wrong wants righting, or a work wants doing, or a truth wants preaching, or a continent wants opening, God sends a baby into the world to do it. That is why, long, long ago, a babe was born at Bethlehem. And that is why, just one short century since, a babe was born at Blantyre. The births column is the only really important one in each day's news.

Mr. Will Crooks told rather a good story the other day. He knew a man, he said, who was always talking about the Empire. He attended every Empire meeting, and joined every Empire league. Every proposal for the expansion or aggrandisement of the Empire he applauded with enthusiasm and vigour. He enlarged upon the glories of Empire at breakfast, dinner, tea, and supper, and on every available opportunity in between. The only drawback about him was that, compared with his imperial visions, his home appeared to him a rather poky place, and he treated his poor little wife with some impatience. One day he arrived before dinner was ready. The baby had been fretful ; the stove had been troublesome ; and everything had gone wrong. The imperial brow clouded, and there was thunder and lightning. The poor wife winced and wept beneath the storm ; and then, smiling through her tears, she went towards her lord, laid the peevish baby in his arms, and said : ' There, now, you mind *your little bit of Empire*, whilst I dish the potatoes ! ' It is a fine thing to dream heroic dreams either of the future Empire or the future Church, but, in order to make those dreams come true, it is just possible that the first step towards it is to look well after the baby.

VIII

THE DOCTOR

JUST over the hill, at the other end of Nowhere, there lives a poor man whose mind is shadowed by a dark and terrible suspicion. He actually wonders whether the Church still retains her ancient gift of healing ! To be sure she does ! As though so precious and beautiful a heritage could ever be really lost ! Let us see how it all happens !

The minister often enters the hushed house. He is admitted by a form on tiptoe, and shown into a front parlour. He sees the doctor's hat and gloves upon the table. He waits for admission to the sick-chamber. He hears at length the bedroom door softly open, and as softly close. There is a whispered conversation in the passage. Then the doctor enters. A formal interchange of common-place greetings takes place between the two men. Then the doctor seizes his hat and gloves, and hurries off. A moment later the rattle of his carriage wheels or the toot of his motor dies away in the distance. They have met and parted without recognizing that they are brothers! That is the pathos of it!

How often they meet, those two! And how little they know of each other! It is a thousand pities. The minister gets into the way of regarding his work as distinctly *spiritual*, and the doctor's as distinctly *physical*. The doctor forms the same bad habit. And so the old, old blunders are perpetuated. They both become the victims of what Mr. Silvester Horne, in his *Life of David Livingstone*, calls ' the *water-tight compartment* theory of life.' As though any man could define the frontier-line at which the physical ends and the spiritual begins! A minister is often called to confront a wan and haggard face, and to hear from quivering lips a story of strange inward darkness and mysterious dereliction. And the greatest and truest comfort that he can give in such a case, oftentimes, is to tell the good creature that her trouble is not spiritual but physical. It is not that the Father's love has failed her, but that her own frame has broken down. The body is jaded. The tissues are exhausted. The nerve has collapsed. She needs a doctor.

And, in exactly the same way, a doctor is often called to deal with a man whose hurt no physician can heal. He suffers from a heart oppressed, a mind diseased, a soul that has got out of gear. Here, for instance, is an extract from the journal of John Wesley : ' Reflecting to-day on the case of a poor woman, I could not but remark the inexcusable negligence of most physicians in cases of this nature. They prescribe drug after drug, without knowing a jot of the matter concerning the root of the disorder. And, without knowing this, they cannot cure. Whence came this woman's pain ? From fretting over the death of her son ! And what availed medicines whilst that fretting continued ? Why, then, do not all doctors consider how far bodily disorders are caused, or influenced, by the mind ? And, in those cases which are utterly out of their sphere, call in the assistance of a minister, just as ministers, when they find the mind disordered by the body, call in the assistance of a physician ? *No man can be a thorough physician without being an experienced Christian.*' John Wesley, as his manner is, puts the case as well as it can be put. There are times when the dentist feels that the trouble is not in the teeth but in the nerves, and he sends his client to the doctor. In exactly the same way, a doctor must sometimes discover that his patient's trouble is not within the scope of his treatment, and, if he be wise, he will invite the co-operation of a minister. These two—the doctor and the minister— cross each other's tracks so frequently, just because

the physical and spiritual realms with which they
deal are so inseparable.   I always like, in this connexion, to think of old Sir Thomas Browne and his
wonderful *Religio Medici*.   ' I cannot contentedly
frame a prayer for myself in particular,' he quaintly
tells us, ' without a catalogue of my friends.   I never
hear the toll of the passing bell, though in my mirth,
without offering prayers and best wishes for the
departing spirit.   I cannot go to cure the body
of my patient but I forget my profession, and cry
unto God for his soul.'   That is very fine.   It shows
how impossible it is for even a very clever doctor,
with his eyes open, to discover the exact frontier
which divides the purely physical from the purely
spiritual.   Humanity is a strange tangle ; and no
man can say where the work of the doctor ends
and the work of the minister begins.   The water-
tight compartment theory breaks down all along
the line.   These obvious facts should bind the
doctor and the minister together in bonds of in-
dissoluble brotherhood.

Pity the poor doctor who thinks that the work
of the minister is purely spiritual !   It is absurd.
Why, an indiscreet minister can nullify the most
skilful treatment of the wisest doctor, or powerfully
fortify the modest efforts of the feeblest practitioner.
Dr. R. S. Mullen, of Clarendon, Iowa, recognized this

in an address which he delivered to ministers not so long ago. ' Give us all the help you can,' he pleaded. ' Let the minister never shake the confidence of a patient. I have often lost a case simply because the sufferer became convinced, in spite of my assurances, that she would not get well. Never, for the patient's sake, find fault with the doctor, nor with the school of medicine he practises. Don't advise him to try another doctor. And never play at being doctor yourself. Avoid standing at the foot of the bed and staring the patient out of countenance. Sit by his side, take his hand, and greet him cheerfully. Let your stay be short, pleasant, and hopeful to the fullest degree. On no account speak of other deaths that have occurred from the same disease. Behave yourself so that, after you have gone, the patient will say to the nurse, ' I am glad he came.' All this is, of course, a frank recognition of the obvious circumstance that a minister's work is much more than merely spiritual. And did not Wellington say that he could have saved hundreds of lives on the battlefields of the Peninsular if only he had had more chaplains ?

No, no, no ! The water-tight compartment theory of life will not work. They once brought a sick man to Jesus. And Jesus said, ' Thy *sins* be forgiven thee ! ' The divine diagnosis revealed the

spiritual malady behind the physical symptoms.
Every discerning doctor knows that the influence
of the minister on the physical condition of the
patient is a very considerable factor in the history of
the case.

And pity the poor minister who thinks that the
work of the doctor is purely physical ! Could anything be more preposterous ? I was the other day
turning over the pages of an English illustrated
paper, and came upon the impressive pictures of the
funeral of the late Lord Lister. Would any one
be silly enough to say that Lord Lister's work
was purely physical ? He saved scores of thousands
of lives. And think what that must have meant to
the world ! Again, we have lately celebrated the
centenary of the birth of Sir James Simpson. The
introduction of chloroform has saved hundreds of
thousands of people from mortal anguish, and a
countless multitude from a gruesome death. And
would any one pretend that Sir James Simpson's
work was purely physical ? It was as spiritual as
the tender and beautiful motives by which it was
prompted. But if, in a moment of uttermost for-
getfulness, some thoughtless mortal were to suppose
that the doctor's task is physical, and only physical,
it would be easy to recall such an one to sanity.
We have all lost ourselves in admiration of Sir

Luke Fildes' masterpiece, ' The Doctor,' and of Mr.
John Collier's ' Sentenced to Death.' No reason-
able man could look for sixty seconds upon the taw-
driest reproductions of those magnificent paintings
without feeling instinctively that the work of a
doctor is much more than merely physical. ' To
me,' says the doctor in a very well-known book,
' to me much has been given to see. My Father has
graciously allowed me to help Him. I am first to
welcome the soul that arrives from Him, and I am
the last to say farewell to those whom He takes back.
What wonder if, now and then, I presume to send
Him a message of my faith and my belief ? '

But if these arguments all fail to compel a more
cordial and brotherly hand-clasp between the doctor
and the minister, when they exchange subdued
greetings on the threshold of the sick-room, I have
another in reserve which cannot disappoint me.
For, if ever I see a doctor looking askance at a
minister, or a minister treating a doctor to scant
courtesy, I shall remind that doctor that the very
first Christian doctor was a minister, and I shall
whisper to that minister that the very first Christian
minister was a doctor. *He* was the first great
preacher and the first great healer. ' God had an
only Son, and He was a Missionary and a Physician,'
wrote David Livingstone from Central Africa to

his brother in Scotland. Yes, *He* was a Minister and a Doctor. And, in His turn, ' He called His twelve disciples together, and sent them to *preach* the kingdom of God and to *heal* the sick. And they departed, preaching the gospel and healing everywhere.' These two God hath joined together. The union is a very sacred and very beautiful one, as the heroic story of medical missions can amply testify. The minister and the doctor are comrades, brothers, partners in the holiest and loveliest service of humanity.

And, now that I come to think of it, I am not sure that the doctor is not even more distinctively representative of the faith than the minister. (I speak of the profession, of course, and not of the individual.) Robert Louis Stevenson used to say that ' the doctor is the flower of our Christian civilization.' For you will find priests and prophets everywhere in every age. But you will only find a doctor—as we use the term—where you find a people touched by the tenderness and pity of the Cross. I am not forgetful of the ministry of medicine under ancient civilizations, from Hippocrates downwards. But reflect for a moment. I have mentioned Lister and antiseptics, Simpson and chloroform. Let us think our way back across the years. Back beyond chloroform ; back among

Dickens' sawbones doctors ; back to the blood-letting practitioners of an earlier generation ; back to the days of the king's touch and similar silly superstitions. And, were we to go back further yet, we should come upon those quiet days when England was very young and very small, when the cowled and corded monk was the sole representative of medical science. And if my patient reader cares to pursue the investigation, he will find that the healing virtues of many of the drugs that our doctors now prescribe were first discovered by those secluded anchorites as they strolled the fields and forests round the early monasteries. But we are out of sight now of the doctor as we know him—the doctor of Fildes' and Collier's masterpieces, the doctor of the type of Simpson and Lister, Broadbent and Treves. The doctor, as we know him, is distinctly, and emphatically, the product and representative of a noble, a gentle, and a generous faith. ' If it had not been for Jesus '—to use Dr. Paton's famous phrase— we should never have seen that strong and sympathetic face, should never have felt that soft and skilful hand. The doctor has evolved as the faith has slowly come into its own. The Church has retained her gift of healing by creating the medical profession as we now know it, and by sprinkling the world with hospitals and asylums. In Myrtle Reed's

Spinner in the Sun she gives us a conversation
between young Dr. Ralph Dexter and his father, the
old doctor : ' Father,' said Ralph, ' it may be
because I'm young, but I hold very strongly the
ideals of our profession. It seems a very beautiful
and wonderful life that is opening before me—
always to help, to give, to heal. I feel as though I
had been dedicated to some sacred calling, some
lifelong service.' ' It's youth,' the old doctor
replies, ' and you'll see the whole thing as a matter
of business later on. In the last analysis, we're
working against Nature's laws. We endeavour
to prolong the lives of the unfit, when only the fittest
should survive.'

Now, the old doctor's laconic contention is the
strongest evidence I could desire. It is the peculiar
charm of Christianity that it shelters the diseased,
the stricken, and the maimed. Under a pagan
economy these must all go to the wall. The law of
the survival of the fittest will work its inexorable
will. But, under the shadow of the Cross, we nurse
and tend them all. We let them marry and have
children. We share their frailties by incorporating
them into the common blood. The race becomes a
joint-stock concern, and we take over the bad debts
of the poorest partners. And, since it is largely
by means of the doctor and his ever-increasing

skill that we do it, he is obviously entitled to be regarded as the peculiar emblem and representative of our Christian faith. Apart altogether from the attitude or character of any individual practitioner, we may well ask : If *his* work is not, in its very nature, essentially *Christian* work, then whose is ?

He sent forth those first disciples two by two. And He sent them forth, as we have seen, to do two things—to *preach* and to *heal*. And, for awhile, each of the twain preached and each of the twain healed. Then they agreed to specialize. ' I will devote all my time and energy to the art of preaching ! ' said the one. ' And I will consecrate all my power and skill to the science of healing ! ' replied the other. And in course of time the first of those two disciples came to be called ' the Minister.' And the second of those two disciples came to be called ' the Doctor.' But they still go, as in the early days, two and two. ' In every place that I have been in yet,' said Piper Tom to Evelina, in the *Spinner in the Sun*, ' there has been a minister and a doctor.' Exactly ! They are inseparable. And that is why they are so often found in the hushed house together. And that is how it comes to pass that, in the tender mercy of her Lord, the Church retains intact her ancient gifts of preaching the kingdom and of healing the sick.

IX

THE ANALYST

WE are all born analysts, and we quickly get to
work. The passion for scientific investigation begins in the cradle. A child glories in taking things
to pieces. He is always at it. He will take a clock
to pieces to find the thing that is for ever ticking.
He will take an instrument to pieces to find the
music. He will take a flower to pieces to find the
fragrance. He will take his mechanical toys to
pieces to find what makes them go. He would
take his mother to pieces, if he could, to find where
all the love and sweetness come from. Those who
have no eye for beauty will mutter a lot of commonplace nonsense about his bump of destructiveness
having been abnormally developed. It is not destructiveness at all. When he discovers that his
investigation has destroyed the very thing that he
was fondly investigating, he will weep over its ruin.
Nothing was further from his thought. He is not a
born iconoclast, but a born analyst. That is all.
His most passionate propensity is the scientific

yearning to resolve a substance into its original elements, to ascertain its component parts, to reveal its ingredients, to take it to pieces. And, though he should live to be as old as Methuselah, he will never quite escape from that analytical propensity. Indeed, it may grow upon him. And, as in the nursery it often led him to the ruin of his best-loved toys, so, in later life, his insatiable craving for taking things to pieces will beguile him into many sorrows before it has done with him. Let us trace the thing a little.

But we must not yet say good-bye to the child in his cot. Watch him! He cries and crows and chuckles and squeals. The causes of his antics and grimaces are among the things that are not dreamed of in our philosophy. And yet, what if he is wrestling with some profound analytical problem? What if the young chemist is already in his wonderful laboratory, and is hard at work at his task of taking the universe to pieces? See! He scratches at his cot and he laughs. He pokes at the counterpane and crows in his furious glee. In his delicious merriment he flings his feet into the air and chuckles audibly. And as the pair of pink pillars appear before his delighted gaze, he scratches at them with all his might and main. And then he screams, as if the foundations of the world had been suddenly shaken. You are amazed at his incredible stupidity in scratching himself, and in straightway crying because it hurts. But what if the incredible stupidity be yours, and not his? What if he be absorbed in an analytical experiment? For experiments in a laboratory are never unattended by some risk. See! He has now divided the entire universe into two parts. He has discovered that there is an essential difference between the cot and the counterpane on the one hand, and the pretty pair of chubby pink pillars on the other. He finds, as a result of his elaborate experiments, that certain things make up the ' *I* ' of this life, and must on no account be scratched ; and that certain other things make up the ' *Not-I*,' and may be scratched without pain. Later on he will pass from this purely physical analysis of ' *I* ' and ' *Not-I* ' to the purely ethical dissection of the ' *mine* ' and the ' *not-mine.*' And, still later, his hungry mind will invade and dissect a still more wonderful world. He will pick up, let us say, Matthew Arnold's *Literature and Dogma*, and, sitting at the feet of the brilliant Oxford Professor, he will learn to make a new analysis. For, says Arnold, all scientific religion amounts in the last resort to a clear distinction between the ' *ourselves* ' and the ' *not-ourselves.*' For here, dwelling within the very body that we scratched in the cradle, is ' a power, not ourselves, that makes for righteousness.' And that power is God! GOD in Us! And when he gets as far as this, our young analyst has begun to take the universe to pieces to some purpose!

And yet, at this very point, his knowledge will lead him into mischief. Knowledge always does. Knowledge is like a lie. A lie requires another lie to cover it. And my knowledge requires still more knowledge to teach me how to use it. It is of no use teaching a child how to handle a knife and how to wield a pen. If you leave it at this, you will find him celebrating his knowledge of cutlery and caligraphy by carving his name on the dining-room table. You must teach him how to use the knowledge you have already given him. In the same way, the inborn faculty of analysis must be educated, or it will play some cruel pranks with him. History affords a shocking example. About three hundred years before Christ a young analyst sprang into existence at Alexandria, Euclid by name. Most school children have heard of him. He spent a good deal of his time in taking things to pieces—triangles, squares, and curves. And at last he actually committed himself to this amazing fallacy : ' *The whole,*' he said, ' *is equal to the sum of all its parts.*' It is a fearful thing when the passion for analysis leads a man into so grave a heresy as this.

' The whole is equal to the sum of all its parts.'
Could anything be more absurd? Take *Paradise
Lost* or *Hamlet* or *In Memoriam* to pieces on this
principle, and you will find that the great classic
simply consists of the twenty-six letters of the
alphabet in an endless variety of juxtaposition.
And would Euclid have us believe that the whole
of *Hamlet* is only equal to the twenty-six letters of
the alphabet? It has often been pointed out that
in Gray's *Elegy* there is scarcely a thought that rises
above mediocrity, and yet the combination and
sequence and rhythm of the whole are such that
we have all recognized it as one of the choicest gems
of our literature. The entire poem is infinitely
greater than the sum of all its parts. Or think
of Tennyson's brook, with its deeps and its shallows,
its whirls and its eddies, its song and its chatter, its
foamy flake and its silvery flash, its graceful windings
among ferns and forget-me-nots, its haunts of trout
and of grayling. Now, the analyst who has not
been warned of the peril of dissection will take all
this to pieces. And he will tell you that it consists
of two parts of hydrogen to sixteen parts of oxygen !
If you hear the wildest statement often enough,
you will come at last to believe it. And this young
analyst has read Euclid's axiom so frequently that
he has really come at last to fancy that it is true !

The whole of the brook equal to the sum of all its parts ! The whole equal to hydrogen and oxygen ! Let our analyst read the poem and see ! Does a lovely tune consist merely of so many notes ? We are irresistibly reminded of Balthazar, the infatuated chemist in Balzac's *Quest for the Absolute*. His poor wife is in an agony of apprehension on his account, and she frets and worries about his perilous experiments. She seeks with passionate entreaty to dissuade him. As he looks into her face he notices that her beautiful eyes are swimming in tears. ' Ah ! ' exclaimed the analyst, ' tears ! *tears !* Well, I have decomposed them. They contain a little phosphate of lime, a little chloride of sodium, a little mucus, and a little water ! ' Now, I happen to know for certain that neither Euclid, nor Balzac's chemist, nor all the cold-blooded philosophers in the universe, could ever persuade any husband or lover in the wide, wide world that a woman's tears contain nothing more than these constituent elements ! It is another of those common cases in which the whole is greater, beyond all calculation, than the sum of all its parts. I wonder that it never occurs to such analysts as these to ask themselves this pertinent question : If a whole contains no more than the sum of all its parts, why should either God or man take the trouble to transform

the parts into a whole?   It would be love's labour
lost, with a vengeance.

But, after all, the analyst will not do very much
harm in the world unless he starts to take *himself*
to pieces.   If he confines his attention to poems, and
books, and tunes, and tears, he may miss a vast
amount of beauty and pathos and music and
romance ; but he may survive that.   The wreck
will not be total.   But when he begins to take
himself to pieces, he will make a tragic mess of
things unless he knows exactly how to go about it.
Here, for example, is an extract from the *Practical
Druggist.*   It tells us that an average man is made
up of so much iron, so much phosphate, so much
salt, so much gas, so much water, and so on.   Now,
does any one feel that this is quite satisfactory ?   Is
this MAN ?   Is the whole only equal to the sum of all
its parts ?   Where does consciousness come in, and
conscience, and passion, and love, and hate, and
everything that makes me ME ?   And is your
analyst much nearer to the truth when he dissects
himself another way, and says that he consists of
spirit and soul and body ?   I think not.   I have
noticed something about the body which is wonderfully spiritual, and something about the spirit which
is wofully carnal.   The analysis is very crude.   I
prefer to take myself as I am—a whole which is

very much greater than the sum of all its parts—
and to cry with Behmen, the mystic : ' Only when
I know GOD shall I know MYSELF ! '

Here, then, we have a most extraordinary
phenomenon. We are analysts from our cradles,
yet we never excel at it. It is the one thing we
begin to do as soon as we are born ; and we are still
doing it very clumsily and very badly when the time
comes to die. We look around us, and we divide
things in general into things *sacred* and things
secular. What could be more stilted, more unnatural, more artificial ? As though to a secular
mind anything could be sacred ! As though to a
saintly soul anything could be secular ! We divide
our fellow mortals up into *saints* and *sinners*. But
we often suspect our own analysis. We find ourselves gazing in admiration at the saintliness of
some sinners ; and we find ourselves in grief at the
sinfulness of some saints.

We turn from things *around* to things *within*, and
soon find ourselves in the same confusion. Chesterton says that the battle of the future is the battle
between the telescope and the microscope. He is
mistaken. The battle of the future is between the
telescope and the stethoscope. And in that fight
the telescope must win. It was fashionable, once
upon a time, for most excellent and devout people

to spend half their time with the stethoscope in awful introspection and analysis. Such self-examination has its place ; but it has been sadly overdone. I prefer to lay down the stethoscope and take up the telescope. ' Looking *off* unto Jesus,' says a wonderful writer who points out this more excellent way. It is so very difficult to analyse the soul and to dissect the good from the bad. I like to think of that great and gracious Covenanter, David Dickson, Professor of Theology in Glasgow University. When he lay dying, he attempted to analyse his inmost self ; but he soon abandoned the attempt. Then, turning to his bosom friend, John Livingstone, who sat beside his death-bed, he said : ' I have taken them all—all my *good* deeds and all my *bad* deeds —and have cast them all together in a heap before the Lord ! I have fled from *both* of them to Jesus ; and in Him I have sweet peace ! ' It was beautifully and bravely spoken. That is the last word in analytical science.

X

THE SCAVENGER

WHO has not lost himself in rapt and reverent admiration as he has stood before A. T. A. Schenk's great picture of ' Anguish ' in the Melbourne Art Gallery ? The dead lamb lying stiff and stark on the bleak and snow-wrapped moor ; the grim circle of coal-black crows perched ominously round, craning their necks and flapping their wings in their impatience to blood their beaks and bury their talons in the banquet that awaits them ; the tell-tale crimson blood-marks that splash the white, white snow ; and, most affecting of all, the distracted mother, with eyes that would move the coldest onlooker to tears, standing sadly over her lifeless lamb, attempting, like Rizpah in the Bible story, to protect her precious charge from the avarice of the hungry birds. It is a pathetic painting ; but it is not with its pathetic side that I propose to deal. I am the champion of the crows. And in order to help me to a better opening of

my case, I propose to lay beside ' Anguish '
another picture of a very similar kind, but in
which the element of pathos is somewhat less
pronounced.

Mr. E. T. Grogan is, as readers of *From Cape to
Cairo* know, the Cambridge undergraduate who
trudged right through Africa from the far north to the
extreme south. ' I envy you,' wrote Cecil Rhodes,
' for you have done that which has been for centuries the ambition of every explorer. The amuse-
ment of the whole thing is that a youth from Cambridge during his vacation should have succeeded
in doing that which the ponderous explorers of the
world have failed to accomplish. There is a distinct
humour in the whole thing. It makes me the more
certain that we shall complete the telegraph and
railway, for surely I am not going to be beaten
by the legs of a Cambridge undergraduate ! ' But
to our picture ! In the course of his trudge Mr.
Grogan shot a zebra, and left it in the bush for lion-
bait. Rising at daylight next morning, he took
his gun, and crept cautiously towards it. ' It would
be difficult,' he says, ' to imagine a more perfect
picture. In the background stretched the limitless
plain, streaked with mists shimmering in the growing
light of the rising sun. Clumps of graceful palms
fenced in a sandy area where the zebra had fallen.

Round its attenuated remains a strange group had gathered. In the centre I saw a grand old lion leisurely gnawing the ribs. Behind him were four little jackals squatting in a row. They were like four little images of Patience, sitting there whilst the lion, in all his might and matchless grandeur of form, leisurely chewed and scrunched the tit-bits. And around these, scarcely out of reach of the swish of the monarch's tail, was a solid circle of some two hundred vultures, craning their bald necks and hustling one another. Loth to break the spell, I watched the scene for fully ten minutes. Then, as he showed signs of moving, I took the chance afforded of a broadside shot and bowled him over. He was a fine black-mane lion, and measured over ten feet— a very unusual length.'

Now, I appear—as the lawyers say in court— for the defendants. I represent the crows in the *first* picture ; I am for the lion, the jackals, and the vultures in the *second*. And I think that I have a particularly strong case. It is not good that the carcase of the lamb should be left to pollute the field. My clients, the crows, did not kill the lamb. But now that it is dead, it is fit and proper that the body should be removed. Otherwise it will vitiate the air, and become a menace to living lambs, and perhaps bring anguish to other fleecy mothers. And so the crows have come to save the lives of those living lambs, and to preserve those other mothers from despair.   They are Nature's undertakers, sent to remove the object that will soon be a festering eyesore and a fruitful source of pestilence and peril. Again, it is not good that this dead zebra should, under a fierce African sun, sow every breeze that blows with the germs of frightful disease, and thus become a plague-spot in a paradise.   And so my clients, the lion, the jackals, and the vultures, as shrewd and sensible sanitary officers, have come to remove a nuisance that threatens the life of both man and beast.   They are God's scavengers—these clients of mine—and, as Frank Buckland, the eminent naturalist, finely says : ' If any creature deserves, more than any other, to be defended and protected, it is that creature which performs the duty of a scavenger.'   And so, gentlemen of the jury, with a very good conscience and with a very strong case, I appear for the crows, and the vultures, and the hawks, and the wolves, and the hyenas, and the jackals, and the sharks, and for all the rest of those unfortunate creatures who, without rhyme or reason, are doomed to live beneath the scowl of mankind, in spite of the fact that they spend their whole time in cleaning up God's world and in making it sweet and wholesome and habitable for the very people who scowl at them.

And, now that I have taken up the case, I shall not be content with a bare verdict of *Not Guilty*. Indeed, I shall be grievously affronted and wounded and insulted if, after presenting my case, I merely secure a verdict of *Not Guilty*. It will not be enough for the judge to inform my innocent clients that they leave the court without a stain upon their characters. The judge and the jury must inform my clients frankly that the court is profoundly impressed by the distinguished services that my clients have for so long, and with so little recognition, rendered to mankind. The judge must turn to my clients, the crows, and he must say, ' The court finds that so far from your having done any injury to this dead lamb, or its poor distressed mother, you and your predecessors actually made life possible for both the lamb and the mother. The court is convinced that had earlier generations of crows not been hard at work in keeping the fields cleansed from all things putrid and corrupt, plagues and pestilences would have annihilated the entire race of sheep long ago. The court desires, on behalf of both men and beasts, to thank you for the valuable services that you have rendered. Indeed, the court feels that, had there been no crows, there could have been no court. The court owes to you, and to those like you, its very existence.' I shall not be satisfied, I repeat, unless my clients—the crows, the vultures, the wolves, and the jackals—leave the court with some such musical words as these ringing in their oft-insulted ears.

I like to think that when the great Lord of all the worlds, who always sees the best even in the worst of us, paid His wondrous visit to this little world, He paid His tribute to the value of the services rendered to humanity by these clients of mine. ' Wheresoever the carcase is,' He said, ' there shall the vultures be gathered together.' ' Horrible ! ' cries some short-sighted ignoramus. But what is horrible ? That is what I want to know. *What* is horrible—the carcase or the vulture ? It is the *carcase* that is horrible. And that is why the vultures set to work to remove it. And the Lord of the birds and the beasts paid His fine tribute to the prompt and effective service that my clients render. ' In the East,' says a well-known writer, ' if any beast of burden falls and dies, though the moment before the whole horizon may have been clear, with not a bird in sight, a stream of vultures suddenly appears as if by magic and crowd round the spot.' And Longfellow, in *Hiawatha*, tells us of the same phenomenon in the West :

Never stoops the soaring vulture
On his quarry in the desert,
On the sick or wounded bison,
But another vulture, watching
From his high aerial look-out,
Sees the downward plunge, and follows;
And a third pursues the second,
Coming from the invisible ether,
First a speck, and then a vulture,
Till the air is dark with pinions.

' Away in the western sky,' says Dan Crawford, in
Thinking Black, ' Lo! a dozen dark vultures
hovering for the funeral of an antelope. The official
mourners these, come to bury a denizen of the plains.
More than mourners, they are the African *grave-diggers*; and more than grave-diggers, they themselves are the *graves*, the *spades* their own beaks.'
Bravely done and bravely spoken! And so the
desert is kept sweet and clean and fresh—the
desert that, but for the vultures, would reek with foul
disease. ' Wheresoever the carcase is, there shall
the vultures be gathered together.' It is a fine
tribute to the skill, efficiency, and promptitude
of my long misunderstood clients!

He—the great Master and Lord—applied it to the
long drama of the world's history. Nations, like
men, die; and empires, like individuals, decay.

And when life is extinct, they become corrupt, pestiferous, abominable. And whenever nations so pollute God's fair world, He has His scavengers at hand to keep the planet sweet. Think of the Canaanitish peoples, with their abominable vices and superstitions ; and the great empires of antiquity that became first voluptuous and then vile. What an imposing and impressive pageant could easily be cited ! The *carcase* is there ; and *therefore*, as it is written, the vultures are gathered together. The fault is not with the birds ; the fault is with the body.

This great saying about the carcase and the vultures is the finest illustration I know of the blending of the divine justice and love. It is out of the divine tenderness that the crows are commanded to cluster round the dead lamb and save other lambs from pestilence. It is part of the divine care that leads the lion and the jackals and the vultures to gather round the dead zebra, and remove from the plain a hot-bed of disease. God's judgements, both in natural history and in human history, take ugly forms ; but they are wonderfully wise and no less wonderfully kind.

Yes, I hold a brief for the crows, and the vultures, and the hawks, and the wolves, and the hyenas, and the jackals, and the sharks, and for all God's scavengers. If it were not for them I should not be here to hold the brief for them; and the jury to which I now so confidently appeal would not be here to hear me. And yet, and yet—even whilst I defend them I confess that I am frightened of them. They are a terrible crowd, these unlovely clients of mine. Even as I defend and belaud them, their frightful fangs, their blooded beaks, their dripping talons, their gleaming tusks, make me shudder. As I lay down my brief I am grateful—profoundly and ceaselessly thankful—for two things. Firstly, I am thankful, even whilst I praise them, that they only bury their hideous faces in that which is putrid and corrupt. The living sheep in the picture does not fear the crows. 'Wheresoever the *carcase* is, *there* shall the vultures be gathered together.' And, secondly, I am thankful—more thankful than words can tell—that I need never become their prey. 'He that believeth,' said their great Lord and mine, 'he that believeth hath everlasting *life*.' 'He that liveth and believeth in Me shall never die.' 'Never die! *Never die!* NEVER DIE!' That is grand! It is a gospel worth preaching. I hurl that great triumphant word into the terrible faces of my ugly clients, and, with a smile on my face and a song in my heart, I leave my case with the court.

PART III

I

GRANNY

GRANNY was a pioneer with a vengeance. When the Free Church of Scotland first announced its intention of establishing a colony in far-away New Zealand, she, her husband, and her young family were among the very first emigrants to be enrolled. *Brave* little woman ! For in those days New Zealand was thought of as the happy hunting-ground of wild barbarians. And *good* little woman ! No finer testimony could be produced to the excellent character that Granny then bore. For the Free Church was determined to send out only men and women of unimpeachable integrity ; and a most searching scrutiny was made into the character of each proposed emigrant. Granny and her guid man stood the test ; and, by the very first ship that sailed for the strange southern land, away they went ! After a voyage of nearly six months, the *Philip Lang* cast anchor off the New Zealand coast. She had been becalmed in the tropics, and had been tumbled in mountainous seas about the Cape ; but she reached her haven at last.

I have often looked at New Zealand from the scene of that historic anchorage, and have tried to conjure up the land as Granny first saw it. No streets; no houses; no shops; no anything! Virgin bush right down to the water's edge! What a gorgeous riot of emerald forestry! The newcomers must hew down for themselves the trees from which their first rude cabins must be built. And I like to remember that, before an axe was raised or a spade lifted, those heroic pioneers and pathfinders kneeled together on the shore and sought grace to lay the foundations of a new nation in the love of righteousness and in the fear of God. Granny was a young woman then, plump and bonny, with her husband by her side and her children at her skirts. If peace hath her victories no less renowned than war, she has her heroes too. And heroines. And surely a Scottish lassie who could accompany her brawny young husband as he carved a path through an untrodden antipodean forest, in order that they might found for themselves a home in the silent and uninhabited interior, has earned a Victoria Cross!

Granny and her husband paused at last on the summit of a mountain, overlooking the blue, blue sea on the one side and a silvery lake on the other. There on the crest of the hill they resolved to build for themselves a home, and to seek their bread by cultivating the bush-clad slopes around. Fifty years later it was often my delight to visit her. I was always dragged up the mountain track on a pair-horse sledge. And I never climbed that steep ascent without thinking of those early days when poor Granny, with no track made for her and no horse to help her, fought her way up the difficult slope as best she could. And I doubt not that she bore her bairnies much of the way, or how could they have clambered through the bush to the summit ? Those first colonists were made of iron. Up there, on the mountain-top, a home was soon built. It was very rough, but it did. The bush was burned and the first crops were sown. And the great lake on which, in those first days, Granny looked down, was drained by companion settlers, and converted into one of the most fertile plains on the face of the earth. It was out on the bed of that old lake that my manse was built for me.

I cherish amongst my richest treasure-trove the memory of my first visit to Granny. She had been recently widowed. Her sons and her grandsons farmed the fertile hill-sides all around her. And they had built for her special comfort a dainty little cottage at the back of the old homestead. The picture is indelible. There she stands in the

rose-covered doorway of the quaint little cabin,
like a pretty old painting, exquisitely framed!
I can still see her wrinkled face buried in the wavy
depths of her lilac sun-bonnet. Her little plaid
shawl is neatly crossed over her breast and fastened
behind her back. Her Scottish accent was so pronounced and her brogue so broad that I cannot pretend to have caught every word that she uttered ;
but for all that it was a treat to hear her. There is
music in the murmur of the waves, though we know
not what they are saying. And at any rate, if poor
Granny's speech was too subtle for prosaic southern
ears, her eyes were always eloquent enough. They
seemed to glow with the very joy of living ; and as
she stands there, framed in her cottage portal, her
hands seem always outstretched to welcome her
minister. I wish that every man could share my
rare privilege in passing straight from college to such
a school as Granny kept for me ! When, nowadays,
I find sleep coy and difficult to woo, I just lie still
and think of Granny as I used to see her at her
cabin-door in those first days of my ministry in
Maoriland.

What times they were ! What tales she told
me as we sat together in her wee but cosy ' but and
ben ' ! The pathos of her early exile ; her in-
sufferable home-sickness as she sat, on quiet and

lonely Sabbaths, her face in her hands and her
elbows on her knees, peering over the wilds and the
waters, dreaming fondly of the auld land and the
auld kirk. How tenderly she told of the patient
struggles of those first days of colonization : the
infinite labour of building their home on the summit ;
the long and perilous tramps in search of every
simplest requisite ; the heavy burdens that had
to be carried on their own backs in the days before
horses and cattle were to be had ; the prosperity
that responded to toil ; and the ease that came with
the years ! Of all these she chatted easily, cheerfully, gratefully.

And when, after awhile, I saw her tall young
grandson pass the open door on his way to the stable
to harness the horses to my sledge, I used to reach
for her old Bible. It had accompanied her through
all the days of her pilgrimage. The covers had been
more than once repaired. Every page was brown
with age and wear. How fondly she eyed it as I
opened its mellow leaves ! I read to her passages
that were like music to her soul. She always chose
them, and her face simply gleamed as I read. She
had learned every word of those stately chapters by
heart before I was born, and, had I stumbled,
would have instantly detected the slip ; but she
enjoyed the passage none the less on that account.

And then **we** kneeled together in the Presence that was very real; and somehow I always felt that prayer was wonderfully easy in the perfumed atmosphere of that little room.

I heard one day that Granny was dying! It was raining in torrents! There was no way of arranging for the mountain-sledge. I drove to the foot of the track, and then commenced the ascent. It was the only time that I ever walked it. And I even felt glad that it was raining. It would have seemed a horrid incongruity if the sun had been shining and the birds singing when old Granny was dying!

To my joy, I arrived in time! Granny was lying dreadfully still and perfectly prostrate in her tiny room. The watchers thoughtfully slipped out and left us, as we had so often been, alone together. I stroked the wrinkled brow about which the snowy curls were tumbled now. Her eyes spoke to me in reply, and I understood. For the last time I reached for her Bible. I knew what to read. If for her great countryman there was ' only one Book ' at such a time, for Granny there was only one chapter. ' In my Father's house are many mansions.' Even as I gave utterance to the beautiful and rhythmic cadences, the rain ceased to beat upon the little window-pane, and I read on amidst a silence that was like the threshold of another world. It was like the hush of the Presence-chamber, the ante-room of the Eternal. I could see that Granny drank in every syllable, and it was as the wine of the kingdom of heaven to her taste. And then I prayed—or tried to—for the last time! When I rose from my knees by her bedside, the setting sun had struggled through the rain-clouds. It streamed gloriously through her little western window. It transfigured her wan face and wandering hair as it fell upon her snowy pillow. I quietly rose to leave. I was about to take her hand in mine when a thing happened that I think I shall remember when all things else have been forgotten.

To my amazement, Granny rose, and sat bolt upright! In the glory of the setting sun, she seemed almost more than human. '*Doon!*' she exclaimed, '*doon!*' and motioned me to kneel once more by her bedside. I obeyed her. And, as I knelt, I felt her thin, worn hands on my head, and I heard her clear Scotch accent once more. 'The Lord bless ye,' she said in slow and solemn tones; 'the Lord bless ye and keep ye! The Lord bless ye in your youth and in your auld age! The Lord bless ye in your basket and in your store! The Lord bless ye in your kirk and in your hame! The Lord bless ye in your guid wife and in your wee bairns! The Lord bless ye in your gaeings out

and in your comings in frae this time forth and
even for evermair ! ' I have bowed my head to
many benedictions, but I have never known another
like that.   The frail form was completely exhausted,
and poor Granny sank back heavily upon her pillow.
In a very little while she had passed beyond the
reach of my poor ministries.   But I often feel her
thin fingers in my hair ; and that last benediction
will abide, like the breath of heaven, upon my spirit
till I shall see her radiant face once more.

II

' WULLIE ! '

WULLIE was my first deacon. That is to say, he was
the senior deacon of my church in Maoriland when
I arrived. It was a great and memorable night
in my life when I met him first. I had been asked by
the college authorities to go out to New Zealand
and be the first minister of the church at Mosgiel.
I consented with a light heart. But the long, long
voyage had opened my eyes to the enormous chasm
that yawned between me and all that I really loved.
Here was I, a stranger in a strange land, an exile
in the uttermost ends of the earth. And it was a
very dejected and miserable and home-sick young
minister who was being borne into Dunedin on the
Christchurch express that night. It was the last
stage of a journey that had seemed interminable.
Or almost the last stage. For at Dunedin I was
to change, and take the suburban train that was
actually to land me in Mosgiel. I sat there in the
express, trying to imagine the people who would
presently meet me—the people who were to be

father and mother and brothers and sisters to me
through the long years to come. A few names had
reached me, and I attempted to conjure up forms
and faces to fit them. It is never a very satisfactory business, and I was not sorry when the
twinkling lights of the city and the wild scream of
the engine announced that we were approaching
Dunedin at last.

I suspected that some of my new people might
be lying in wait for me here, and I was not mistaken.
As the train slowed into the brightly-lit platform,
I caught a glimpse of a group of eager and inquisi-
tive faces anxiously scanning every carriage. I was
soon in the midst of them, receiving a most gracious
welcome. They were all kindly and reassuring ;
but of all those honest and homely faces one stood
out from among the rest. It was one of the simplest, and yet one of the saintliest, faces I have ever
seen. What ruggedness was there ! And yet it was
luminous, for it fairly shone ! It was a winsome face,
and mischief twinkled in those eyes. It belonged
to an elderly little Scotsman. My dejection thawed
beneath his smile. All loneliness vanished. In
some occult way of his own he made me feel that I
was trusted and honoured already. His wrinkled
face beamed ; his bright eyes sparkled ; and his
speech faltered through deep emotion. Lookers-on

might have been pardoned for supposing that I was his son. I had dreaded that night's experience as the greatest ordeal of my life. He dispelled the illusion and turned it into a home-coming. I was among my own people. One man at least loved me, and that man was Wullie. ' Puir laddie ! ' he said, as he reflected on my long voyage to a strange folk.

I have said that I was the first minister at Mosgiel. That is scarcely true. Wullie was the first minister. He was the father of them all. It was a very well-worn track that led to Wullie's door. The young people confided their love affairs to Wullie ; the older people poured all their troubles into his sympathetic ear. He was pastor and peacemaker. I always think of Wullie when I recall that great saying in *Ecce Homo* : ' The truth is that there has scarcely been a town in any Christian country since the time of Christ where a century has passed without exhibiting a character of such elevation that his mere presence has shamed the bad and made the good better, and has been felt at times like the presence of God Himself. And if this be so, has Christ failed ? or can Christianity die ? ' No ; Christianity is safe as long as there are men like Wullie about.

And yet I *was* the first minister after all. I learned afterwards how Wullie had set his heart on

having a minister at the church. He had thought
about it, talked about it, and prayed about it until
it had become the one fond dream of his old age.
At every church meeting he rose and wistfully
referred to it. Were the members quite sure that
the time was not yet ripe ? And when at last, with
great trepidation, the church yielded to his impor-
tunity, and committed itself to the formidable proposal, Wullie's delight broke all bounds. How
impatiently he had awaited the letter from the
English college ! How excitedly he had spread
the great news that a minister was actually coming !
How he had pored day by day over the shipping
news for any fragmentary tidings of the vessel that
bore me ! I could understand all this afterwards in
the light of the welcome he gave me.

Four months later, on Wullie's motion, of course,
the church decided to terminate the temporary
character of my appointment and to call me to its
permanent pastorate. On my acceptance the good
people presented me with a cosy arm-chair. Wullie
was appointed to make the presentation. He read
his speech. He could not trust himself that night
without manuscript. His heart was full. I shall
never forget his tenderness and enthusiasm. I
little dreamed that Wullie was addressing us all
for the last time.

Nor was it quite the last time. For Wullie's last speeches—if single sentences can properly be classified as speeches—were delivered at a church meeting. If I must enter into details of a distinctly domestic order, the church was in financial difficulties. I do not mean that they had not enough money. I mean that they had too much. The one overpowering dread of these cautious Scots folk had been lest they should lure a young minister all the way from England and then find themselves unable to support him. This horror had alone constrained them, through many years, to postpone the realization of Wullie's darling dream. And when the minister was actually there, the fear became still more acute, with the result that the members contributed with frantic munificence. The exchequer was overflowing, and the poor treasurer was at his wit's ends.

' If the church get to know that we've got all this money,' he exclaimed in despair, ' the collections will drop off to nothing ! '

This was at a deacons' meeting. It was generally agreed that in some way or other the money must be spent, and each man undertook to try to think out the best means of disposing of it.

But their plans were all shattered. At the church meeting held a few days later one of the

members, little dreaming that he was precipitating
a crisis, asked for a financial statement. The treasurer slowly rose. He was the picture of abject
misery. Anguish was stamped upon his face. He
could not have looked more forlorn or wobegone had
he stood convicted of misappropriating the church
funds. He confessed, with the countenance of a
culprit, that he had fifty pounds in hand! The
position was appalling !

But at that fateful moment Wullie, as his custom
was, sprang into the breach and saved the situation.
He rose deliberately, a sly twinkle in his eye, and
quietly asked :

' Would the meenister tell us if he has a lassie ? '

I was covered with confusion, and I buried my
face to hide my blushes. I confess that, for two
minutes at least, I lost control of that meeting.
But, happily, my very confusion saved me the
necessity of a reply. My secret was out. Wullie
was on his feet again.

' Then, Mr. Chairman,' he said, with the gravity
of a statesman, ' I move that we buy a piece of
ground with that fifty pounds, and that we build
the meenister a manse.'

The resolution was carried with enthusiasm.
The treasurer looked like a man who had been
saved from the very brink of destruction.

The manse was built, and it was for many years
my home.   It had but one discomfort, and that was
the sorrowful reflection that poor Wullie never lived
to see either the manse or its mistress.   One Saturday afternoon, as we were all preparing for an
anniversary celebration on the Sunday, without a sickness or a struggle Wullie suddenly
passed away.   We were thunderstruck.   It was
incredible.   I have rarely seen grief so general and
so sincere.

Wullie had some queer little ways.   Among his
peculiarities was this :   When he went to the pay
office at the factory and drew his weekly wage, he
always looked the coins carefully over with a keen
and critical eye, and laid aside the bright ones for
the church collection.   ' The Lord must aye hae the
best, ye ken ! ' he used to say.   He could not bear
to put a worn or battered coin upon the plate.
At a crowded memorial service, at which the
whole countryside turned out to do honour to his
memory, there fell to me the heavy task of preaching Wullie's funeral sermon.   I referred to this
habit of his with the coins.   It was so eminently
typical and characteristic.   ' If,' I said, ' I were
asked to suggest a suitable epitaph to write above
his grave, I should inscribe upon the stone these
words :   " HERE LIES A MAN WHO ALWAYS GAVE

HIS BEST IN THE SERVICE OF HIS SAVIOUR ! " '
And he who visits the pretty burying-place on the
outskirts of Mosgiel at this day may easily find the
green spot where Wullie sleeps, and read that faithful
record engraved above his head.

III

A CANARY AT THE POLE

Yes, a canary at the Pole! Or, at least, next door to it. For the tiny songster of whom I write is the canary that I found on board the *Fram*. His cage hangs in the men's quarters. Right in front of him, not more than a yard away, are the photographs of King Haakon, Queen Maud, and little Prince Olaf. All the cabins open into this diminutive saloon, so that his song can easily penetrate every chamber and cheer every man. And I was told by one of the explorers that this golden chorister, who, as his name implies, belongs to one of the softest and sunniest climates on the face of the earth, never sang with more gaiety and abandon than when the ship was in the midst of the ice. Brave little bird!

I remember visiting on three occasions the Canary Islands. I was there once in January, once in May, and once in September. But, whatever the month, it seemed always the same. There appeared to be but one season. Summer reigned through all the year. Tropical vegetation clothed

the hills.   What soft, delicious skies !   How balmy
and luxurious the spice-laden air !   How rich and
voluptuous the long, lazy, starlit evenings !   And
this is the home of my little canary !   A world
which winter can never invade ; a paradise in which
every breath is laden with the odour of luscious
fruit and the fragrance of delicate flowers !   And
then to think of the South Pole !   Piercing winds,
nipping frosts, driving snow-storms, continents of
ice, and snow-drifts that have piled themselves in
glaciers and frozen into mountains !   One shudders
to think of it !   It was all very well for sinewy
Norsemen, hardened by a sterner and more rigorous
climate, to steer their barque into these icy seas.
They had made friends with the biting wind, the
blinding sleet, and the paralysing cold.   And,
moreover, they could suit their wardrobe to their
new conditions.   What furs and wraps and strange,
ungainly dresses !   But a *canary* at the Pole !   Ugh !

And the beauty of it is that he sang there, and
sang out bravely his very blithest songs !   Like
Browning's ' wise thrush,' he

> sings each song twice over,
> Lest you should think he never could recapture
> The first fine careless rapture !

That is beautiful !

Here, then, is a gospel for all exiles. This tiny
chorister on the *Fram* puts to shame the record of
the captives in Babylon : ' *By the rivers of Babylon
there we sat down, yea, we wept, when we remembered
Zion. We hanged our harps upon the willows in the
midst thereof. For there they that carried us away
captive required of us a song : and they that wasted
us required of us mirth, saying, " Sing us one of
the songs of Zion." How shall we sing the Lord's
song in a strange land ? '*

It was quite otherwise with our little canary.
They that carried *him* away into captivity required
of *him* a song, and, in a stranger land than Babylon,
amidst snow and ice, he gave them of his best.

If I had time and strength, I should like to write
to all our missionaries and tell them this story of
the canary at the Pole. I am sure it would help
them to sing their sweetest songs in strange lands.
They are lonely in the midst of the great multitudes.
There is no loneliness so cruel as that. I shall never
forget the day when, at the age of sixteen, I left
home and found my way to the roar and rattle and
din of London. I had never seen such crowds anywhere, jostling and pushing for every inch of pavement. And yet I remember standing that day
in the heart of the world's metropolis, under the
very shadow of St. Paul's, and shivering in the thick

of the crowd at my own utter loneliness. Amid
the hops and the clover and orchards of my Kentish
home, one could often shout to his heart's content,
and never a soul would hear him. Yet that was a
delicious and tranquil loneliness that one loved and
revelled in, but the loneliness of that awful surging
crowd seemed an intolerable thing. And it is just
that loneliness, in a much more acute form, that
oppresses our missionaries on cannibal islands in
southern seas, among the hordes of Central Africa,
in the bustling bazaars of India, and amid the
myriads of inland China. Sunday comes, but the
Sunday atmosphere comes not. There lies the
hymn-book from which they are singing ' Rock
of Ages,' ' Sun of my Soul,' and all the dear old
melodies in the churches and chapels at home ! But
how can *they* sing the Lord's song in a strange land ?
I would not presume, even if I could, to preach a
sermon to a real live missionary ! I would just
tell him about the canary at the Pole. And then
I fancy that, just as one bird sets all the forest singing and floods the glades with music, so my little
canary would start the praise of a thousand lonely
outposts. And the neglected hymn-books in the
Mission stations would soon become worn with
constant use.

Not that missionaries are the only people in the

world who should be told of the *Fram's* canary. By
no means. A young man tells me that the office in
which he earns his living is such an uncongenial
place for the development of the religious life. I
dare say! The Pole is not particularly congenial
to a canary! But he sang there for all that. A
young lady tells me that it is simply impossible
to be a Christian in her workroom! Really! And
I should have thought it simply impossible to be a
canary at the Pole! But it isn't! And if a canary
can sing a throat-splitting song at the Pole, surely a
Christian can contrive to maintain his testimony in
the most chilling and disheartening atmosphere.

I cannot imagine what the canary was singing
about down there at the great ice barrier. I don't
know why he sang. I can only suppose that he sang
just because he was a canary, and, being a canary,
could not but sing. And I fancy that a Christian,
just because he is a Christian, will find some way of
expressing—naturally, acceptably, delightfully—the
best life that is in him, even in the most nipping and
chilling circumstances.

But the point is that the gaiety of our canary's
note was all the more delightful and effective because
of the frigid conditions amidst which he sang. He
might have split his throat in his soft and sunny
northern home, and yet never have cheered a soul.

But to sing in the midst of the ice ! That was fine !
It was heroic, and everybody blessed him. It was
the one sublime opportunity of his lifetime; he
seemed to know it, and he rose to the great occasion.

Of course ! Any one can sing when the sun shines.
But here's a benediction on those brave spirits whose
song holds on through grey and gloomy days ! Any
one can sing in summer ; but give me the bird that
can be blithe on bare and dripping boughs, surrounded by a wilderness of winter. Any flower can
preserve the purity of its pretty petals when
hemmed in by green lawns and well-kept walks ;
but the whiteness that I most admired was the
snowy blossom that grew in a coal mine, where
the grimy dust was flying all day long !

Yes, it is at the Pole that we most prize the song
of the canary. The testimony of a gracious life is
no more conspicuous in a prayer-meeting or a communion service than the note of a canary at Madeira.
We accept it as our right. We take it for granted.
But piety in a factory where the moral atmosphere
is many degrees below zero ! Devotion in an office !
Holiness in a workroom ! ' Saints in Caesar's
household ! ' It is under just such conditions that
religion has an opportunity of becoming famous.
It is at the Pole that a canary can distinguish himself. It is *there* that his song really tells !

IV

HAIRBREADTH ESCAPES

THE loss of the *Titanic* will always be spoken of as one of the world's most thrilling and dramatic tragedies. Mr. L. Beesley, until lately Master of Science at Dulwich College, has written a picturesque and vivid volume telling in graphic detail the story of that fearful night. He describes his own wonderful escape from the ill-fated ship, and instances also many of the hairbreadth escapes of his fellow passengers. And this has set me thinking. For it seems to me that hairbreadth escapes have a philosophy of their own. All through life hairbreadth escapes are the only things we really care to hear about or read about. If you find a boy curled up in a cosy chair, absorbed in a book, you may be perfectly certain that his flushed face and flashing eyes betoken an exciting stage of a hairbreadth escape. The hero has just succeeded in scaling the prison wall, or he has just broken from a fierce tribe of Red Indians, or he is flying for his life from a horde of cannibals. Or—to take life at its other end—if you chance to find the arm-chair occupied by the boy's grandfather, and are happy enough to catch him in a garrulous mood, he will at once plunge into the story of his hairbreadth escapes. Even Paul, in writing to Corinth, succumbed to this inevitable tendency. It is ever so. And, just because it is ever so, the three most popular books in the language are simply crammed from cover to cover with astonishing records of hairbreadth escapes. I refer, of course, to the Bible, to *Pilgrim's Progress*, and to *Robinson Crusoe*.

Look, for instance, at the Bible. Here are Lot's escape from Sodom, Isaac's escape from the altar, Joseph's escape from the pit, Israel's escape from Egypt, Moses' escape from Pharaoh, Elijah's escape from Jezebel, David's escape from Saul, Jonah's escape from the deep, Jeremiah's escape from the dungeon, the Hebrew children's escape from the burning fiery furnace, Daniel's escape from the lions, Peter's escape from prison, Paul's escape from shipwreck, John's escape from exile, and very many more. Did ever book contain so many astounding adventures? Then Bunyan's immortal classic is all about Christian's escape from the City of Destruction, his escape from the Slough of Despond, his escape from Apollyon,

his escape from Vanity Fair, his escape from
the Flatterer's net, his escape from Giant Despair,
his escape from the Valley of the Shadow, and his
escape from the waters of the river. And as for
Robinson Crusoe, there is a hairbreadth escape on
almost every page.

The same argument holds good if we turn from
biblical biographies to those of later times. The
most impressive passages are the hairbreadth escapes. John Wesley never forgot his deliverance,
as a child, from the burning parsonage. ' The
memory of it,' his biographers tell us, ' is still preserved in one of his earliest prints. Under his por-
trait there is a house in flames, with this inscription :
" Is not this a brand plucked out of the burning ? " He remembered this remarkable event ever
after with the most lively gratitude, and more than
once has introduced it in his writings.' Everybody remembers Dr. Thomas Guthrie's miraculous
escape on the cliffs of Arbroath, John Knox's extraordinary deliverance in rising from his study chair
a second or two before it was shattered by a bullet,
John Howard's wonderful escape from the hand of
the assassin, and George Washington's similar
adventure at White Plains. And as to David
Livingstone, Mr. Silvester Horne tells us that, besides his historic escape from the lion, he sometimes

met with as many as three positively hairbreadth
escapes in a single day. I suppose the true inwardness of such escapes, and the element about them
that has most profoundly moved us all at some time
or other, was never better expressed than by the
wild and dissolute Lord Clive. Thrice he attempted
suicide, and thrice the revolver unaccountably
refused to do his awful will. At the third failure
he flung the weapon down, exclaiming, ' Surely
God intends to do some great thing by me that
He has so preserved me ! ' And he became the
victor of Plassey and the founder of our Indian
Empire.

But life has most wonderful escapes, quite apart
from pistols and precipices, from floods and flames.
Mr. H. G. Wells contributed a very striking article
to the *Daily Mail* the other day, in which he em-
phasized the modern tendency to escape. ' The ties
that bind men to place,' he writes, ' are being
severed ; we are in the beginning of a new phase
in human experience. For endless ages man led
the hunting life, migrating after his food, camping,
homeless, as to this day are many of the Indians
and Esquimaux in the Hudson Bay Territory.
Then began agriculture, and for the sake of securer
food man tethered himself to a place. The history
of man's progress from savagery to civilization is

essentially a story of settling down.' Then Mr. Wells goes on to show us how the tide turned. The day of the traveller dawned. Railway trains, motor-cars, *Mauretanias*, *Titanics*, aeroplanes, and cheap fares became the order of the day. Migration is the watchword of the world. The earth has, almost literally, a floating population. ' The thing is as simple as the rule of three,' Mr. Wells concludes. ' *We are off the chain of locality for good and all.* It was once necessary for a man to live in immediate contact with his occupation, because the only way for him to reach it was to have it at his door, and the cost and delay of transport were relatively too enormous for him to shift once he was settled. Now he may live twenty or thirty miles away from his occupation, and it often pays him to spend the small amount of time and money needed to move—it may be half-way round the world—to healthier conditions or more profitable employment.'

Mr. Wells' article is the story of a great escape. Men do not now live like poor Tim Linkinwater, sleeping every night for forty-four years in the same back attic ; glancing every morning between the same two flowerpots at the dingy London square, and convinced that nowhere in the world was there a view to rival that landscape ! No ; we have escaped, and we keep on escaping. It becomes a

habit. Every holiday is an escape, often a hairbreadth escape.

' There is one person from whom you *must* contrive
to escape,' said Doctor Sir Deryck Brand to Lady
Inglesby, his patient, in Mrs. Barclay's *Mistress of
Shenstone.*

' One person——? ' queried Lady Inglesby.

' A charming person,' smiled the doctor, ' where
the rest of mankind are concerned, but very bad
for you just now ! '

' But whom ? ' questioned Lady Inglesby again ;
' whom can you mean ? '

' *I mean Lady Inglesby !* ' replied the doctor
gravely.

And Lady Inglesby soon learned the joys of a
hairbreadth escape, for, from the seaside inn at
which she stayed *incognito*, she wrote :

' It was a stroke of genius, this setting me free
from myself ; the sense of emancipation is indescribable ! '

Every composure of a weary head upon a soft
pillow is an escape, a breaking loose from the cares
that relentlessly pursue, an immigration into the
land of sweet unconsciousness or radiant dreams.
Every indulgence in really refreshing recreation is
an escape. Every pleasure is an escape. I noticed
that the theatrical editor of the London *Graphic*, in

the issue that was crowded with pictures of the coal strike, headed his page ' A Way of Forgetting all About the Strike.' ' In all good deer forests,' he wrote, ' there is a sanctuary—to which the deer can retire with complete immunity—not because their lord and master is philanthropic, but because he knows that, if he shoots everywhere in his land, the deer will cross the border into his neighbour's demesne and probably not return. At such a moment as the present—the great industrial war being in full swing—we all need a sanctuary to which we can retire from the rumours of war, from strikes, from newspaper jeremiads, and from all other depressing influences. The retirement is not an act of cowardice. It is necessary as a resuscitation. It helps one to get on the top of things, to see life in perspective, and with some sort of common sense.' From such a source, that passage is wonderfully suggestive. 'A way of forgetting!' 'A sanctuary!' ' A retirement ! ' The man who has found this way of forgetting, this sanctuary, this retirement, has *escaped*—that is all.

Or think what an excellent means of escape a really good book represents. ' Is your world a small one ? ' asks Myrtle Reed. ' Is it small and made unendurable to you by a thousand petty cares ? Are the heart and soul of you cast down by bitter

disappointment? Would you leave it all, if only
for an hour, and come back with a new point of
view? Then open the covers of a book!' And
we have all fallen in love with Mr. Edward Thomas'
village scholar in *Horae Solitariae*. 'He finds a
refuge from the shadows of the world among the
realities of books.' He set his little cabin door
between the restless world and himself, wandered
across to his bookshelves, and felt a supreme pity
for plutocrats, plenipotentiaries, and princes!

Nor is this all. For in Mark Rutherford's
Deliverance the genial and lovable philosopher says
a very striking thing. In the poky little window of
a small undertaker's shop in a London slum he saw,
between two dismal representations of hearses, a
rude cross. It powerfully impressed him. 'The
desire to decorate existence in some way or other,'
he says, 'is nearly universal. The most sensual
and the meanest almost always manifest an indis-
position to be content with mere material satisfaction. I have known selfish, gluttonous, drunken
men spend their leisure moments in trimming a bed
of scarlet geraniums, and the vulgarest and most
commonplace of mortals considers it a necessity
to put a picture in the room or an ornament on the
mantelpiece. The instinct, even in its lowest
forms, is divine. It is the commentary on the text

that man shall not live by bread alone. It is evidence
of an acknowledged compulsion—of which Art is the
highest manifestation—*to escape.'* The italics are
his, not mine. In the rude cross that adorned the
shabby and gloomy window, Mark Rutherford saw
a hint of an exit, a way out, an escape. Just as the
geraniums and the pictures are an escape from the
sordidness and ugliness and bareness of London
squalor, so the cross in the undertaker's window
pointed a way of emancipation to aching and breaking hearts.

Now, this is leading us very near to the heart of
things. For surely the Christian Church, with her
atmosphere of charity and purity and peace, is a
most gracious and grateful escape. And even death
itself, by the time that it comes, is to most people
a gentle and welcome deliverance.

But I really believe that, after all, the finest thing
ever said or sung about an escape is that blithe note
of one of Israel's sweetest singers. ' *We are escaped !'* he sings as he looks back upon the Captivity. ' The snare is broken, and we are escaped !'
It is like the gay outburst of the birds in an English
grove whilst the torn meshes of the nets around bear
witness to the perils from which, with ruffled
plumage, they have lately been delivered.

' *We are escaped !'* cried the Jews as they

exultantly re-entered Jerusalem, and gave way to transports of gratitude and delight. ' The snare is broken, and we are escaped ! '

' *We are escaped !* ' cried old Theodore Beza, his hair white with the snows of eighty winters, as he went up to the ancient church at Geneva after the long agony of persecution and oppression was past. ' The snare is broken, and we are escaped ! '   And every year, on the anniversary of that historic proclamation of three centuries ago, the great psalm is chanted by the people gathered in the same building.

' *We are escaped !* ' cried William Knibb, as he announced to the slaves of Jamaica the victory of the Abolitionists. ' The snare is broken, and we are escaped ! '

' *We are escaped !* ' cried the dying McCheyne. In the collapse of the body, a strange darkness had overtaken him. He asked to be left alone for half an hour. When his servant returned, his face was radiant and his voice triumphant. ' I am escaped ! ' he exclaimed. ' The snare is broken, and I am escaped ! '

Said I not truly that it was like the melody of birds in a sweet English grove whilst the torn and tangled snares lay all around ? ' The comparison of the soul to a bird is beautiful,' says Dr. Maclaren.

' It hints at tremors and feebleness, at alternations of feeling like the flutter of some weak-winged songster, at the utter helplessness of the panting creature in the toils. One hand only could break the snare, and then the bruised wings were swiftly spread for flight once more, and up into the blue went the ransomed creature, with a song instead of harsh notes of alarm : We are *escaped* ! we are *escaped* ! we are *escaped* ! '

Dr. J. H. Jowett, of New York, told the other day the story of a dream. A friend of his dreamed that he was a hare, with the hounds in hot pursuit. They were rapidly overtaking him, and he could feel their horrid breath as they drew nearer. Presently, as he reached some bare and rocky heights, he discovered that, instead of hounds, they were his own sins that chased him, and that he was a flying soul. Far up towards the summit of the hill he saw a cave, flooded with a most unearthly light. At the entrance there shone resplendently a Cross. He hurried to it, and, as he reached it, the hideous things that had pursued him slunk dejectedly away. He awoke and knew it was a dream. But the dream led him to the Saviour. And it led him to the Saviour because he saw that, of all life's miraculous and hairbreadth escapes, the escape by way of the Cross is by far the most wonderful and by far the most amazing.

V

ESCAPES—*NOT* HAIRBREADTH

I RETURN to the matter of escapes, suggested by
the remarkable stories of the survivors of the
Titanic, and, on thinking it all over again, I have
reached the deliberate conclusion that my own
escape was as wonderful as any.

In *The Six Gates* the Rev. T. Thomson, M.A., tells
this excellent story : ' Some years ago,' he says,
' a steamer going from New York to Liverpool was
burned at sea. A boatload of passengers succeeded
in leaving the ship, and were saved. Among them
was a minister belonging to Dublin. When he returned from his ill-omened voyage, he was the hero
of the hour, and told his thrilling story far and near
with great effect. He used to dwell especially on the
signal mark of God's favour he had received. So
many had perished ; yet he was saved ! It was a
marvellous and special providence that had so cared
for him and preserved him. He never told his story
without dwelling on this aspect of it, the uncommon
mercy of God. One day he was recounting his

strange experience to a company of people, among whom was the great Archbishop Whately. When he came to the end, and made the usual remarks about the extraordinary providence that had snatched him from the burning ship, Whately turned to him and said, " A wonderful occurrence ! A great and signal mercy indeed ! But I think I can surpass the wonder of it with an incident from my own experience ! " Everybody pricked up his ears and listened for the passage in the Archbishop's life which should show a yet more marvellously merciful escape than that of the minister from the burning ship. Whately went on in the expressive manner for which he was celebrated : " Not three months ago I sailed in the packet from Holyhead to Kingston " —a pause, while the Archbishop took a copious pinch of snuff, and his hearers were on the tip-toe of expectation—" and by God's mercy, *the vessel never caught fire at all* ! Think of that, my friends ! " ' The point is a good one. Said I not truly that, of all the wonderful escapes from the *Titanic*, my own was as notable as any ?

Hairbreadth escapes are enormously popular. These better escapes are not. Nobody in the room really felt that Archbishop Whately's escape was more wonderful than that of the Dublin minister. Nobody really believes that my escape from the

Titanic was more remarkable than Mr. Beesley's or Colonel Gracie's. We are too fond of a thrill. We love the things we don't like. We all remember Darwin's story of the monkeys and the snake. A snake in a paper bag was inserted in the monkey-cage. The curiosity of the animals led them to unfasten the top of the bag and peep in. When they saw the reptile they rushed screaming up the bars of the cage, and huddled together at the very top. But they could not stay there. One would come down, peep at the snake, scream, and rush away. Then another. And another. They could not leave it alone. They loathed it and loved it at one and the same time.

The same peculiar instinct is in us all. We go a long way, and pay a good deal, to see a man in peril of his life. If he will fling himself from a balloon in mid-air, or insert his head in a lion's mouth, or walk a tight-rope over a roaring cataract, or swing by his toes at a dizzy height, the crowds will rush to see him. Now the question is : Do the people who pay to witness these sights really wish to see the performer killed ? It is perfectly certain that they would not pay their money if the element of danger were absolutely eliminated. Make it safe, and no one wants to see it ! Why, then, does the crowd throng the building ? Do the people really cherish

a secret and terrible hope that the parachute will not
open, that the lion will sever with his dreadful teeth
the keeper's neck, that the rope walker will miss his
footing over the surging waters, that the acrobat
will slip and fall from his lofty trapeze? No, it is
not that; for the great sigh of relief is distinctly
audible when the fearful peril has been safely
negotiated. It is nothing more or less than the
innate and morbid love of a hairbreadth escape. In
some form or other this extraordinary passion
characterizes us all. But it is totally illogical and
unreasonable. The escapes of which I am now
writing are infinitely better.

There is a quaint old poem which Professor
Henry Drummond, in his *Ideal Life*, turns to fine
account. It is entitled 'Strife in Heaven.' It
imagines the glorified spirits to be discussing which
of them all is the greatest monument of redeeming
grace. Each tells his story. Vote after vote is
taken. At length only two competitors are left
in the contest. The first of the two is a very old
man whose whole life had been spent in the most
diabolical wickedness. Yet, at the eleventh hour,
on his death-bed, he was forgiven. It was a hairbreadth escape. His rival was also an old man.
But he was led to Christ when quite a little boy,
and had been saved from all the sins which the other

had committed.   The vote was taken, and all heaven
acclaimed the second competitor the winner.   ' The
one,' says Henry Drummond, ' required just one
great act of love at the close of life ; the other had
a life full of love—it was a greater salvation by far.'
The one was a hairbreadth escape ; the other was
an escape of a very much finer sort.

Every minister knows that there are no questions
more frequently presented to him than those relating
to questionable pastimes or amusements.   ' Is there
any harm in this ? '   ' May I play at such and such
a game ? '   ' Is it right to go to such and such a
place ? '   ' Is it wrong to take part in this, or that,
or the other ? '   It all arises from our insensate craving for hairbreadth escapes.   Even children love
to walk on the edge of the kerb, to creep near the
brink of a precipice, and to lean far out of a high
window.   But why run the risk ?   The story of the
Canadian pilot is very threadbare.   But it is very
much to the point.   ' Do you know,' asked a nervous
passenger, ' do you know where all the rocks and
reefs and sandbanks are ? '   ' No, madam ! ' the
skipper bluntly replied.   The passenger was just
preparing for the inevitable hysteria, when the
captain saved the situation by adding, ' But I know
where the deep water is ! '   Just so.   Nobody wants
a pilot who cruises about rocks and reefs, avoiding

them only by the skin of his teeth.   But the captain
who, knowing very little of such terrors, is certain
of the deep waterways, is a very safe skipper
indeed !

Our modern evangelism is in peril of collapse
at this very point.   We often glorify hairbreadth
escapes, and, by inference, minimize the value of
escapes like mine from the *Titanic*.   I mean to say
that we glorify guilt and belittle the preciousness of
innocence.   In one of his best books Professor
W. M. Clow has a fine passage on the blessedness of
a life which has nothing to forget.   ' There is a tendency,' he says, ' which hectic modern literature and
morbid preaching are emphasizing, to think that the
man or woman who has not had a wild and wayward
outburst in the days of youth is a poor, pale-blooded
creature.   There is a feeling that the man or woman
with a dark story behind is more piquant and interesting, and that a youth of blameless innocence merg-
ing into a life of saintly purity, as the dawn merges
into the full day, misses the romance of life, and
knows nothing of any high elation of spirit such as
he feels who spurs into reckless sin.   There seems to
be with some the impression that a rake makes the
finest saint, that his devotion has a richer and deeper
colour than that of the unspotted soul ; and that
even the girl who has had a frivolous and rebellious

youth shall mellow into the wisest and kindest
womanhood.   Surely this is one of the wiles of the
devil.'

Of course it is !   I like to think that Jesus had
a place in His great heart for the woman who was a
sinner and the thief on the cross by His side.   I like
to remember that the guiltiest things that breathed
found room in His infinite love and absolution from
His pure lips.   But I like to remember also that
it was when Jesus met the rich young ruler, who had
kept all the commandments from his youth up, that
it is written that ' He, looking upon him, loved him.'
Jesus never taught that the greatest escapes were
the hairbreadth escapes.

On a memorable public occasion the late General
Booth was stepping from his carriage to enter a well-
known public building.   As he did so a drunken man
staggered stupidly towards him, and in scarcely
intelligible accents exclaimed, ' Say, General, what
are ye going to do with the like o' me ? '   The crowd
gathered quickly round to hear the General's
answer.   The General laid his hand on the drunk-
ard's shoulder, and replied, ' My friend, we can't do
much for you ; but we're after *your boy* ! '   That
is a piece of very sage philosophy which I commend
to all parents and teachers.   Hairbreadth escapes
are very difficult to compass.   There are escapes that

it is much more easy to bring about. And those easier escapes are the best escapes after all.

Nobody has enjoyed more than I have such books as *Broken Earthenware, Down in Water Street, Mending Men,* and the rest. They are great and heartening reminders that a man is never beyond redemption as long as a breath is left in him. But there is a peril lurking even in such admirable literature. The escape of old Born Drunk is not anything like so lovely a thing as the consecration of a child. Mr. Begbie, Mr. Hedley, and Mr. Smith have told us of thrilling and hairbreadth escapes. They are very, very wonderful ; and we thank God for every one of them. But the young fellow who yields his unstained manhood to the service of the Saviour ; the girl who brings to the feet of her Lord the lovely offering of her sweet and gracious womanhood—these present a still nobler spectacle. Hairbreadth escapes are splendid, simply splendid ; but, after you have unfolded their most thrilling story, a still more wonderful tale remains to be told.

VI

PRAYING FOR CARLO

I CAUGHT myself looking in at a bookseller's window
the other day in a perfunctory and absent-minded
kind of way, when I was suddenly pulled up with a
start.   The good man was offering a quantity of his
old stock at greatly reduced prices.   One shelf was
even marked ' Sixpence,' and it certainly contained
a lot of rubbish that would fetch no more.   But half-
way along the shelf I saw, to my amazement, Mr.
Edwin Hodder's *Life of Sir George Burns, Bart.*   It
was the original large type edition, with fine steel
engravings, absolutely new and with pages uncut.
No man in his sober senses would allow a biography
of any kind to linger in such humiliating conditions.
But a volume by Mr. Hodder—the author of the
standard biographies of Lord Shaftesbury and of
Samuel Morley !   And least of all would any sane
man permit Hodder's *Life of Sir George Burns* to
continue in such desperate straits.   Sir George
Burns was, of course, the founder of the Cunard
Steamship Company.   He was, therefore, to all

intents and purposes, the father of the modern
ocean liner and the pioneer of our huge oceanic
traffic. We have recently celebrated the centenary
of the first passenger steamship (whose first voyage,
by the way, Sir George Burns witnessed), and the
volume has a peculiarly timely interest. Moreover,
Sir George Burns was the son of Dr. Burns, and
the intimate personal friend of Dr. Thomas Chalmers,
Dr. Thomas Guthrie, and of the other stalwarts of
the great Disruption days. And Sir George holds
the unique distinction of being the oldest baronet
ever created, for it was at the age of ninety-four
that, to his almost boyish exultation, Queen Victoria
conferred his well-earned title upon him. I need
scarcely say that I returned to my home that afternoon with sixpence less in my pocket, but feeling
very amiably towards myself and the world in
general.

I have since read this fascinating story from
cover to cover with unflagging interest and delight.
It sparkles with matters of paramount interest ; but
one stands out from the rest. It is of that one
characteristic that I now write. Sir George was a
Presbyterian of the old school. The Church, the
Sabbath, and the family altar were his chiefest
treasures. He had unlimited faith in prayer. But
the thing that has impressed me has been the

admixture of sanity with spirituality. I give one example :

In its early days the Cunard Company had to contend against fierce—almost frantic—competition. For a while, some of the opposition boats contrived to beat the Cunarders in the race across the Atlantic. But Sir George Burns refused to be discouraged. He saw his records beaten ; he heard the murmurs of his supporters and the cheers of his rivals ; but he persisted in his policy of building ships that were first safe, and then swift. Everybody told him that the faster ships would soon run his own off the Atlantic ; but he smiled knowingly, and quietly went his own way. He considered speed in each order that he sent to the yards ; but he considered safety first. Then came the crisis. In September, 1854, the *Arctic*, one of his opponent's fleet of four steamers, foundered at sea, with fearful loss of life. The wife, son, and daughter of the proprietor went down with the ship. In a little more than a year, the *Pacific*, the second of the opposition ships, followed suit. She left Liverpool, and was never heard of again. The prestige of the rival company was in ruins ; whilst the Cunard Company was still able to advertise that it had never lost a passenger. The loss of the two vessels of the one company and the absolute immunity of

the other set many tongues wagging. Some com-
mented upon the Cunard Company's ' wonderful run
of luck.'   Others talked about a ' special interposi-
tion of Providence ' on behalf of the Cunarders.
Indeed, there was a story current that the sailing
of every ship of the Cunard fleet was made the subject of special prayer, and that Mr. Burns was wont
to attribute his success to this source.   Mr. Burns,
however, would never recognize this as the true
interpretation of the position.   He held that there
were certain elements that made for the safety of a
vessel, and that these elements were within human
control.   He was scrupulously careful in providing
his ships with all these features even if he sacrificed
speed, risked his profits, and invited public censure
by doing so.   ' I believe implicitly,' he would say,
' in the power of prayer ; but I also believe in doing
work well, and in subordinating profit, and speed,
and public opinion to safety, comfort, and efficiency.'
The difference between his boats and those of his
rivals was not that his boats were more prayed for
than theirs, but that their construction was more
carefully guarded.   He did not believe that Providence could be persuaded by the prayers of any one
owner to favour his particular commercial enterprise
to the detriment and disadvantage of others.

Now, this is very suggestive. But I have not

finished with Sir George Burns yet. I propose to
follow him from his busy office to his beautiful home.
Castle Wemyss is a lovely mansion, built upon a
huge rock at the extreme edge of the promontory
where the River Clyde widens into the Firth. It is
one of Scotland's most palatial but delightful
homes ; and Sir George was accustomed to entertain
there ladies and gentlemen of the highest rank and
station. But, whoever was there, Sir George always gathered the entire household every evening
about the family altar, and always personally con-
ducted the worship. On one occasion, Mr. Hodder
tells us, Sir George's dog—a great favourite—was
lost, and his master mourned for him. The most
diligent search was made ; and when at last it had
to be abandoned as hopeless, Sir George's grief was
pitiful to behold. And when the old man bowed
himself that evening in the midst of his household,
and led them to the Throne of Grace, he included
an affecting petition for his wayward collie. ' *O
Thou*,' he prayed, ' *who preservest both man and
beast, and without whose knowledge not a sparrow
falls to the ground, we pray that, wherever our old
friend and companion may wander, it may please
Thee to find him a home among folk by whom he will
be well received and kindly treated !* ' I hope to read
a good many more books in my time ; but I expect

to meet with few more charming touches than
that.

And now I have finished with Sir George Burns.
But, in this matter of the Cunarder on the one hand
and of Carlo on the other, Sir George has drawn my
attention to a matter of the utmost significance and
importance. We ministers are for ever and for ever
telling our people that they ought to pray. We preach
that wholesome doctrine to the point of weariness.
But we rarely point out that it is often very wrong
and very wicked and very dangerous to pray. And
it certainly is. Sir George Burns makes it clear
to me that I must not pray for my Cunarder unless
I have exhausted all the faculties of wit and skill and
ingenuity in securing her safe construction. It is
wrong to pray for Carlo unless I am taking good
care that no stone is left unturned in the search
for him. Now, I fear that, in preaching this doctrine, I may shock some most excellent people whom
I would not shock for all the world. I must therefore fortify myself. Let me lay beside these stories
of Carlo and the Cunarder three classical illustrations—two of a positive and one of a negative kind.

1. Moses shall be my first. ' And the Lord said
unto Moses, Wherefore criest thou to *Me*? Speak
unto the Children of Israel that they go forward.'
It was no time for prayer. The Egyptians were at

their heels. The sea was in front. The army had been commanded to march. But Moses prayed. And God rebuked him for praying. ' Wherefore criest thou to *Me*? Go forward ! ' It was no time for prayer ; it was time for progress. It was no time for meditation ; it was time for movement. Dr. Adam Clarke, the great commentator, was a slow worker.   And he could only produce his wealth of literary treasure by long and patient toil. He therefore made it his custom to rise early every morning. A young preacher, anxious to emulate the distinguished doctor, asked him one day how he managed it. ' Do you pray about it ? ' he inquired. ' No,' the doctor quietly answered ; ' *I get up ! '* Mr. Moody used to tell how once he came upon a group of wealthy American Christians praying for the removal of a debt of one hundred pounds on their church building. ' Gentlemen,' said Mr. Moody in his incisive way, ' I don't think if I were you, I should trouble the Lord in that matter ! '

Now, I confess that this great word in Exodus often alarms me. I am a minister, and I find myself praying for my people.   I am a father, and I find myself praying for my children. And sometimes I fancy I hear a voice breaking in upon my supplications and asking, ' Wherefore criest thou unto *Me*? Speak unto *them* ! ' We have already seen that I

have no right to pray for my ships until I have done
all that human forethought can effect to render them
safe and seaworthy ; we have seen that I have no
right to pray for Carlo unless I have scoured the
whole neighbourhood in search of him. And now I
see that I have no right to pray for my people unless
I am putting all my conscience and all my soul into a
full and faithful ministry ; and I have no right to
pray for my children unless I am, by my lips and by
my life, labouring ceaselessly to lead them to the
Saviour's feet. ' Wherefore criest thou unto Me ?
Speak ye to the children ! ' I never read that text
without thinking of Susanna Wesley. Was there
ever a mother like that mother of the Wesleys ?
One night she had been praying for her great family.
' At last,' she says, ' it came into my mind that I
might do more than I do. I resolved to begin. I
will take such proportion of time as I can best spare
every night to discourse with each child by itself.'
How Susanna Wesley kept that good resolution, and
with what tremendous and earth-shaking results, the
whole world very well knows.

2. My second illustration is the story of Balaam.
Balaam saw his duty with perfect clearness. And
instead of doing it, he prayed about it. And disaster
followed. Nothing could have been more specific
than his instructions : ' God said unto Balaam, thou

shalt not go with the men ; thou shalt not curse the people.' Yet, in defiance of that clear commandment, he prayed for guidance ! 'The fault of Balaam,' says Dr. R. A. Watson, ' was that of tampering with his inspiration. He has a clear mind, a clear eye ; and his way is plain. Yet the withdrawal of his mind from its sole allegiance to God tells at once on his moral vision. It is clouded. The oracle becomes ambiguous. He hears two voices, many voices, and his mind is confused. He takes a crooked course.' And he suffers shipwreck. Balaam's great sin was the sin of praying. He prayed himself into the conviction that he might do the very thing that he had been specifically commanded not to do. If my duty is once made plain to me, my duty is to do my duty, and not to pray for a guidance that has already been most clearly vouchsafed.

3. The negative illustration that I promised is the case of Philip. ' The angel of the Lord spake unto Philip, saying, Arise and go toward the south, unto Gaza which is desert. And he arose and went.' Sensible man ! And successful man ! If he had stopped to pray about it, he would have missed the Ethiopian's chariot. The angel said, ' Go ! ' He arose and went ! And by going promptly he just met the chariot as it swept past on

the sandy road. After the angel had said ' Go ! ' it would have been both wicked and disastrous for Philip to have paused to pray for guidance. It would have spoiled everything.

Yes, there is a time when it is right to pray. We must teach the people that. But there is a time when it is *wrong* to pray. And we must teach the people *that*. I have no right to pray unless, by sweat of brain and brow, I am doing my utmost to compass the end for which I pray. I confess to a fondness for that fine story which General Booth was so fond of telling. The General knew of a little girl who worried herself into a fearful state of agitation concerning the birds that became entangled in her brother's traps. One evening, at her mother's knee, she prayed about it. ' O Lord,' she prayed, ' don't let the little birds get into Robbie's traps ! Please don't let them ! ' And then, to her mother's astonishment, she added exultingly, ' Oh, I know they won't ! They can't. Amen.' ' But, Dolly,' remonstrated her mother, ' what makes you so sure that God will answer your prayer for the birdies ? ' ' Why,' exclaimed Dolly confidently, ' 'cause, before I prayed, I went out into the garden and *smashed the traps* ! ' There is a world of very sound philosophy to be gleaned at that point.

VII

MOUNT DISAPPOINTMENT

HAMILTON HUME was the first of that gallant band
of ' overlanders ' of whose splendid exploits Australians are so justly proud.   He it was who led the
first pathfinders from Sydney to Melbourne.   In the
course of that tedious and historic pilgrimage, there
were two great and memorable moments, one of
exultation and one of depression.   The first was
when Hume, on ahead of the party, suddenly
stopped, waved his hat in boyish glee and came
running back to announce to his comrades his discovery of the Murray.   The other was when, exhausted and famished, they sighted the mountains
that we know as the Hume Range.   The party were
worn out, and begged to be allowed to give up and
return.   Hume pointed to a mountain ahead of
them.   ' From that summit,' he assured them, ' we
shall see the ocean, and shall go back and tell of our
success ! '   The mountain was climbed ; ' but when,
after a desperate struggle, they reached the top,
nothing met their eyes but miles and miles of ridges

and gullies covered with trees'; they named it
'*Mount Disappointment*,' and, to their everlasting
credit, pressed on and safely reached their goal.
It is not the only episode of the kind that glorifies
those early days. What shall we say of Burke, and
Wills, and King as they stagger into the camp at
Cooper's Creek, after their long trudge across the
dusty heart of the continent, only to find the camp
forsaken and death staring them in the face?

Many of us have never crossed the Hume Range;
but we have clambered up Mount Disappointment
for all that. Perhaps of all disappointments, the
disappointments of childhood are the most bitter.
I know a home in a city. I saw it one Christmas
Eve. What romp and revelry! What excitement
and clapping of hands! What gay decorations and
graceful festoons! What suggestions and specula-
tions! How would Father Christmas come? And
when would he arrive? And what would he bring?
How carefully all the stockings were hung up—
especially baby's! But that night father met with
some boon companions. Little sleepers, already
restless with excitement, were still further disturbed
at midnight by unsteady steps and clumsy noises.
And then, at dawn, nervous little fingers clutch
eagerly at the pendant stockings, only to find them
as empty as ever. And whilst little fingers are

grasping at empty stockings, little feet are making
their first pilgrimage up the slopes of Mount Disappointment. A full stocking cannot contain so much
of bliss as an empty one can hold of bitterness.

Again, I know a home in the country. It is a
farmhouse, miles and miles from everywhere. There
is a little blue-eyed, flaxen-haired bit of innocence
there, who often sits out by the big white gate,
looking along the endless road that loses itself
at last over the ridge ; and she wonders as she
sits there what the great world is like to which
the long road leads. This morning things are early
astir. ' Daisy ' is harnessed to the spring cart,
for father is going to town ; and in the evening
he will bring Blue-eyes a beautiful doll from
the wonderful store in the city. Oh ! what excitement all day ! Blue-eyes can scarcely eat. Long
before father can possibly have got to town she is
straining her little blue eyes in looking along the
endless dusty road to see if there is any sign of
' Daisy ' and the spring cart. What questions
mother has to answer about that wonderful doll that
is coming ! And at last, far off, there appears a
speck over the ridge. Blue-eyes is sure that it is
' Daisy '—and dad—and dollie ! And so it is !
Clever little Blue-eyes ! At least, it is ' Daisy ' and
dad. But dollie ! Dad had forgotten ! Blue-eyes

does not understand all about the merchants, and the markets, and the warehouses, and the bank, and the rest of the jargon that had worried her father and banished the wonderful doll from his mind. Blue-eyes only knows that there is no dollie after all! Poor, sobbing, broken-hearted little Blue-eyes! Blue-eyes is climbing for the first time the rugged slopes of Mount Disappointment.

Yes, Mount Disappointment is a hard, hard mountain to climb; yet its stony slopes are always crowded. The trying examination that was so nearly passed; the coveted situation so nearly gained; the hoped-for competency so nearly made; the buried love so nearly a bride! And think of the inexpressible disappointments of womanhood, and motherhood, and widowhood! It is hard to climb a mountain heavily laden at any time; and the aching and breaking hearts of these sorrowful mountaineers are the heaviest loads of all. And the worst of it is that it is very difficult to know what to say to these climbers with their torn hands, their bleeding feet, and heavy loads. It seems the veriest cant to tell them that it is all right; that it is all for the best; that everything will turn out happily after all; that it is better not to be able to see the blue waters from the lofty peak; that the little fingers are richer with their empty stockings than they would have been had those stockings been bursting with treasures ! And fancy telling poor little Blue-eyes that she is better without her doll !

Perhaps the best way of dealing with these people is to tell them of some of the pilgrims who have passed this way before them. Some very distinguished travellers have had to climb Mount Disappointment at some time or other ; and, just because they were distinguished, their records come to be written ; and so it comes to pass that we can tell how it all turned out. Perhaps if all the undistinguished people had left their records too, we should find that they had fared just as bravely. Who can tell ?

Here is a famous story to begin with. Oliver Cromwell—then unknown to fame—and John Hampden once climbed Mount Disappointment. Sick and tired of the absurdities of Charles the First, the two cousins resolved to emigrate. The *Mayflower* had left Plymouth seventeen years earlier, and a prosperous little Puritan commonwealth had sprung up across the Atlantic. A vessel, bound for North America, was lying in the Thames. Hampden and Cromwell booked their passages, and were actually on board, waiting for the good ship to sail. At the last moment came messengers from the king, forbidding the two would-be emigrants to leave the country. Charles little knew that, by signing that order, he was signing his own death-warrant. Hampden and Cromwell stepped ashore, *bitterly disappointed*. And that bitter disappointment gave Cromwell to England, and shaped the whole course of our imperial history.

Oliver Goldsmith climbed Mount Disappointment. In 1756, after having obtained a doctor's degree, he found himself without a shilling in his pocket. ' He pounded drugs,' Macaulay says, ' and ran about London with phials for charitable chemists.' Then he aspired to the unambitious post of mate to a naval hospital. He presented himself at Surgeon's Hall as an applicant for the position. To his great chagrin, he was rejected. The record in the college book reads : ' James Bernard, mate to an hospital ; Oliver Goldsmith found not qualified for ditto.' He was *bitterly disappointed*. In his disappointment he seized a pen and began to write. Eight years later *The Vicar of Wakefield*—one of our very greatest classics—was given to the world. ' Genius '—to use Mr. W. J. Lacey's words—' transmuted Goldsmith's disappointment into a golden service to English letters.'

William Wordsworth knew what it was to climb Mount Disappointment. In 1792, the French Revolution being at its height, he visited Paris. He was in his twenty-second year, and the blood of the

September massacres was scarcely dry. He was an
impulsive boy when, as Rosaline Masson puts it,
' rudderless, and under full sail of impetuous feel-
ings and vain hopes, he tossed upon that dangerous
sea. He even entertained and dallied with the
notion that he himself might become leader of the
Girondists ! ' But the heroic dream ended igno-
miniously. To his intense humiliation and disappointment, his uncle stopped his supplies ! That
is putting it rather prosaically. He himself reduces
it to poetry :

> Dragged by a chain of harsh necessity
> So seemed it—now I thankfully acknowledge,
> Forced by the gracious providence of Heaven—
> To England I returned, else (though assured
> That I both was and must be of small weight,
> No better than a landsman on the deck
> Of a ship struggling with a hideous storm)
> Doubtless, I should have then made common cause
> With some who perished ; haply perished too,
> A poor mistaken and bewildered offering,—
> Should to the breast of Nature have gone back
> With all my resolutions, all my hopes,
> A poet only to myself, to men
> Useless.

And thus, as Mrs. Masson puts it, ' the patriot of
the world descended, penniless and reluctant, from

his Paris attic, and returned, crestfallen and disappointed, to England ; and the laureate Wordsworth was saved to literature.'

But I need not multiply illustrations. Everybody knows of the great disappointment of Charles Dickens in missing an opportunity of going on the stage. Everybody knows of Nathaniel Hawthorne's dismissal from the Customs House. Everybody knows of Lord Tenterden's misery at being defeated by a rival candidate for a chorister's place ; and everybody knows of Mr. Spurgeon's disappointment in relation to his application for admission to college. And therefore everybody knows that Charles Dickens' disappointment enriched our literature beyond all possibility of calculation ; that Hawthorne's dismissal from the Customs House did almost as much for our American cousins ; that Lord Tenterden's rejection as a chorister gave to the British Law Courts one of their most distinguished judges ; and that Mr. Spurgeon's humiliation proved a turning-point in a life for which millions glorify God !

That is the beauty of Mount Disappointment. Those first ' overlanders ' did not see the ocean, as they had hoped to do from its summit, but, as they afterwards discovered, they were on the right road. They were never so near to their destination

as when they stood on its blunted peak. Mount
Disappointment lay in their track and brought
them nearer to their goal. That, I say, is the beauty
of our disappointments. Half the ironical and
cynical nonsense that is written about the difference
between the anticipation of marriage and the experience of marriage is written in ignorance of this
great fact. It is true that a pair of lovers look
towards marriage as a roseate romance. It will be
to them an endless courtship, a perpetual honeymoon. And, afterwards, seen from without, it
appears to have been all an illusion. There is constant anxiety ; there is a struggle for a livelihood ;
there are sick children and heavy sorrows. But get
into their hearts, and as they look back upon those
days when they walked hand in hand, and built
romantic castles in the rainbow-tinted air, ask if
they have *really* been disappointed. Marriage has
meant to them an infinitely sweeter thing than the
thing of which they used to dream, and it has left
upon their characters a stamp of nobility that the
realization of their sentimental mirage could never
have produced.

Pretty much the same thing happens in relation
to our faith. To a young convert, religion is all
romance. It is all emotion, rapture, and spiritual
transports. As life goes on, and his devotion works

its way into all the stern realities of a workaday
world, it becomes less and less a thing of catchy
choruses and poetical phrases. But, with the loss
of the sentimental side of faith, he gains a certain
inward grandeur that gives a depth to his thought
and feeling that he never knew before, and that
imparts to all who know him an impression of
sterling dignity and splendid uprightness.

I knew a fine old man who had two sons. The
sons were not Christians ; and the father, as he drew
near to the gates of the grave, used to pray that he
might die a death of such peace and tranquillity
that his sons would be compelled to offer Balaam's
entreaty : ' Let me die the death of the righteous,
and let my last end be like his ! ' The old man
sickened, and the sons were sent for. As the father
neared the borderland, his brain became confused,
and his body racked with pain. His death-bed
was really a terrible affair. Now, here is a poor old
pilgrim climbing Mount Disappointment with the
death-sweat on his brow. Yet see what happened !
The sons argued that if their father, being the saint
that he was, found death so dreadful, things would
go hardly with them at the last. And they kneeled
by their father's death-bed and set out on pilgrimage.

And so Mount Disappointment is a wonderful

place. In its modesty and self-depreciation it tricks us simple-minded pilgrims into the impression that we are on the wrong road. But it is all right. Hume, travelling by way of Mount Disappointment, found the ocean after all. The honeymoon couple lost the glitter, but they found the gold. The convert lost the outward glamour, but he found the inward glory. Cromwell and Hampden, Goldsmith and Wordsworth, clambered up Mount Disappointment in the path of destiny. The fact is that the painful climb up the stony slopes of Mount Disappointment is God's own wonderful way of bringing us into His Promised Land.

VIII

SECOND-CLASS PASSENGERS

I AM travelling saloon, and between the ample and commodious promenade on which I stroll and the small and poky deck on which the second-class passengers disport themselves there is a barrier, and over that barrier is a notice, clearly inscribed in glaring capitals.   Here it is :

NO SECOND-CLASS PASSENGERS

ALLOWED BEYOND THIS BARRIER.

I am writing to insist that that wholesome regulation should be rigidly enforced.   I want no second-class passengers strutting on my deck.   And I think I can make out my case without qualifying for the inclusion of my name in the Book of Snobs.

I fancy I notice a tendency in modern preaching to exaggerate the importance of scientific opinion. It seems to be taken for granted that the conclusions of eminent scientists and celebrated philosophers give to the faith a sanction and an authority

that it would not otherwise possess. I am not prepared to accept the assumption. Scientists and
philosophers, considered *as* scientists and philosophers, are distinctly second-class passengers, and
they must be kept on their own side of the barrier.

Now, I must carefully protect myself, or I shall
be most grievously misunderstood. I speak with no
disrespect. I raise my hat to every scientist and
philosopher living, and to the memory of every
scientist and philosopher dead. The human race
flowers into perfection when a thinker is born.
' Beware,' says Emerson, ' when the great God lets
loose a thinker on this planet. Then all things are at
risk. It is as when a conflagration has broken out
in a great city, and no man knows what is safe or
where it will. end.' Among them that are born of
women there hath not arisen a greater than a
brilliant thinker, a daring philosopher, a distinguished
scientist. *Notwithstanding*, he that is least in the
kingdom of heaven is greater than he. That is to
say, that, great as he is, he is but a second-class passenger after all. It is good, of course, for all who
can possibly manage to do so—and it is almost
essential for every minister—to read what these
princes of thought and peers of intellect have to say.
What a wealthy inrush of mental enrichment has
reached us just lately, for example, through the

brilliant unfoldings of Eucken and Bergson ! All this is most excellent. I do not object to *my* having the right—as a saloon passenger—to go down to the second-class deck and to chat with any passengers I may happen to find there. My protest is against *their* being allowed to invade *my* preserves. I can snap *my* fingers at the barrier. But I protest against *their* being allowed to do so !

I am always delighted, naturally enough, when an eminent thinker avows himself a Christian, just as I am delighted when a crossing-sweeper avows himself a Christian. And, since the thinker may wield his Christian influence over a wider area than is open to the crossing-sweeper, I may, perhaps, rejoice even more in the conversion of the philosopher than in that of the crossing-sweeper. But that is about as far as it goes. I have never felt free to parade the opinions of scientists and philosophers on distinctly religious subjects because I have never felt that they are authorities on those subjects. For one thing, it does not seem quite fair to do so. It happens that, at this moment, the general consensus of scientific and philosophical thought is most strongly favourable to the faith. But I am conscious of very little elation on that account. Nor do I feel that, on that account, my position as a Christian teacher is appreciably strengthened.

And for this reason : Suppose the tide happened to turn ! The very suggestion seems absurd. But the present cordiality between the scientist and the theologian is quite a fresh development. It has grown up in a single century. There is nothing to *guarantee* its permanence. Let us suppose, however ridiculous the supposition may seem, that the general consensus of scientific and philosophical thought became once more strongly sceptical. Should I feel correspondingly depressed ? Should I feel that my position as a Christian teacher was appreciably weakened ? Not a bit of it ! It would not affect a single emotion in my soul, or a single inflection in my voice. ' We preach Christ crucified.' And

> Whatever record leap to light,
> *He* never can be shamed.

And just because I should, in that grotesquely supposititious case, go on with my work as though nothing had happened, it seems to me scarcely fair or seemly to be unduly elated at the sympathetic smiles of our great thinkers, or to assume that my message gains in authority through their endorsement.

The fact is that we have a faith that cannot be shocked by the contempt of these second-class passengers, and which, therefore, derives no real support from their corroboration and patronage. For there is always this difference between those passengers beyond the barrier and myself. They must always speak with hesitation, whilst I speak with unwavering assurance. They are always subject to correction and revision, whilst my certainties are absolutely final. ' *I know* whom I have believed.' ' *I know* that nothing can separate me from the love of God.' ' *I know* that all things work together for good.' ' *I know* that, if my earthly house be dissolved, I have a house eternal in the heavens.' This is the aristocratic phraseology of a saloon passenger, and I mean to be very cautious lest I allow my vocabulary to be corrupted by the men from the second-class. It is interesting, of course, and—up to a certain point—reassuring, that they are saying nothing in their second-class quarters that is in conflict with the things we talk about on our promenade. But then, we talk about lots of things on our deck that they of the second know nothing at all about. Or, to put it quite accurately, we talk of lots of things on our deck that they would know nothing at all about unless we sometimes strolled down to their quarters and discussed these loftier matters with them. What would science or philosophy, left to themselves, have discovered about Sin.

about Regeneration, about Forgiveness, about
Redemption, about Justification, about Eternity?
Or even about God? For science and philosophy
never find God. They merely find *evidence* for the
existence of a God. It is the offer of a stone to a
child crying for bread. For who wants *evidence*?
I want God. Science and Philosophy find His footprint on the sand, as Robinson Crusoe found the
footprint on his island. But who wants a footprint? Would the footprint of his lady satisfy a
lover? No, no, no! He wants her. I want no
footprint. I want *Him*. ' Oh, that I knew where
I might find *Him*!' This is the throbbing cry of
my hungry soul. I want *Him*—Himself. And
neither Science nor Philosophy could ever have
introduced *Him* to me.

The trouble about these second-class passengers
is their insatiable passion for proving things. Their
very facility for proving things proves at least one
thing. It proves how insignificant the things are
that they are for ever proving. We on the first
deck rarely trouble about proving things. For you
can only prove things that do not really matter.
You can never prove the big things of life on which
our very existence and happiness depend. No man
can prove that his mother loved him. No man can
prove that his wife is true to him. Yet no man

would wish to linger on after his faith in these things had deserted him. No man can prove that he has been divinely loved, and redeemed, and forgiven. But his faith in this blissful experience is the joy of his heart and the light of his eyes. On the other hand, those second-class passengers *can* prove that the three angles of a triangle are equal to two right angles, and that two and two make four. But I fancy that I could still eat a decent meal, and sleep with perfect serenity at night, even if my confidence in *these* things should be in some strange way disturbed.

I drew a rather unkind analogy just now between the scientist and the crossing-sweeper. I was half ashamed of it as it trickled off my pen. But now that I come to reconsider the matter, with a view to a possible apology, I am more inclined to apologize to the crossing-sweeper. For it is quite possible that, in the things which we discuss on the first-class deck, the crossing-sweeper may be a higher authority than the philosopher. Professor A. W. Momerie asks himself, in his *Origin of Evil*, why some scientists find the vision of God so blurred and indistinct. ' I think,' he says, ' the chief reason is this. Just as the *body* may be over-trained, and its powers developed to the injury of the mind, so the *mental faculties* may be over-educated—educated, that is at the expense of the spiritual. This has been the case with a good many modern physicists. Their whole lives are spent in weighing, measuring, and analysing things, so that they feel hopelessly lost in regard to subjects which do not admit of such treatment.' And we all recall Darwin's pathetic and classical confession : ' My mind seems to have become a kind of machine for grinding general laws out of large collections of facts.' ' My soul is dried up,' he says again, ' and the very nature of my work has caused the paralysis of that part of my brain on which the highest tastes depend.' And Tyndall stoutly maintained that the devotion of the powers to scientific investigation rendered a man *less,* rather than *more,* competent to deal with theological questions.

There are, of course, times when we lose sight of the scientist in the saint, and of the philosopher in the believer. The Rev. John Morgan, of Fountainbridge, visited Sir James Young Simpson during his last illness. He asked him one day, ' What do you consider your greatest discovery ? ' ' On the morning of Christmas Day, 1861,' the great doctor replied, ' I discovered that I was a sinner, and that Jesus Christ was my Saviour ! ' And Lord Kelvin, when asked by a student which of all his wonderful discoveries he considered the most valuable, startled

his questioner by replying, ' To me the most valuable
of all the discoveries I have ever made was when I
discovered my Saviour in Jesus Christ ! '

But when a man starts to talk like this, I always
discover a first-class ticket peeping out of his pocket ;
and as I stroll the promenade in his delightful company, I no more think of him as a scientist than I
think of Bunyan as a tinker.

IX

THE POPPIES IN THE CORN

I AM writing here in Australia, but in fancy I am standing once more by the old signal-station at Beachy Head ! Even as I scrawl the title across this sheet my mind romps across the years to the happy old times on the wind-swept Sussex downs. They were crowded hours of glorious life when we, as boys, left our lovely inland home behind us, and went off, our faces flushed with excitement, to spend a week by the waves. The delight of hearing once more the song of the surge, of scampering at low tide among the shells and the sea-weed on the strangely crinkled sands ; of splashing and bathing in the restless surf ; of watching the dense black crowd as it roamed about the pebbly beach ; of hearing the nigger minstrels and seeing Punch and Judy from the promenade ! These raptures were transporting enough ; but they were scarcely greater than the exhilarating experience of climbing over the great undulating downs, and of beholding, up on the hills there, the glorious golden cornfields all bespangled

with the bravery of their flaring scarlet poppies.
The man who has once seen the brilliant blossoms
flash out, like flames, from among the bowing ears
of corn, and then vanish again as the waves of gold
surged up around them, will carry with him to his
dying day the vivid memory of that lovely scene.
Kingsley says that very often, in the course of a
quiet stroll through the sequestered English fields
all the leaves and the grasses and the birds seemed
to be calling out to him, but he felt a sense of
humiliation and embarrassment at being unable to
discover what they were saying. As I stand to-day
beside this poppy-strewn cornfield, I should dearly
love to catch its message, and to pass it on. Surely,
surely, surely so altogether fascinating a phenomenon
must have some wonderfully beautiful interpretation. If only I could find it !

I must call to my assistance a naturalist, perhaps
the most mystical and in-seeing of all naturalists.
I have just been reading all the works of Richard
Jefferies, *The Gamekeeper*, *The Poacher*, *Field and
Hedgerow*, and the rest. It has been a perfect
revelry. He has several things to say about the
poppies. But he only once tries to interpret them.
The poppies, he thinks, stand for genius. ' There is
genius in them,' he says, ' the genius of colour ; and
by their genius they are saved.' The interpretation

does not satisfy me ; but it gives me a clue, and I
shall follow it. The poppies in the corn represent
the brilliant among the commonplace. ' The world's
wealth,' Carlyle tells us, ' is in its original men. By
these and their works it is a world and not a waste.
Their memory and their record are its sacred
property for ever.' Mr. G. K. Chesterton, in his
Victorian Age in Literature, lifts his hat respectfully
to the men whom he eccentrically calls ' The
Eccentrics '—Coleridge and Lamb, Leigh Hunt and
Landor, Hazlitt and De Quincy. By ' The Eccentrics ' Mr. Chesterton meant precisely what Carlyle
meant by ' The Originals.' They both meant the
poppies among the corn. Now, this sounds very
nice. It makes us all feel that it is good to be a
poppy. I can imagine dreamy young men and
sentimental young ladies fancying that they already detect the spark of genius sputtering within
their brains. But let us examine the poppy a little
more closely. ' Every one who has gathered the
beautiful scarlet poppies,' Richard Jefferies tells us
in another volume, ' must have noticed the perfect
Maltese Cross formed inside the broad petals by the
black markings.' Now we have made a grim discovery ! Here is the terrible secret of the poppy !
It conceals a cross ! And the cross is in its heart !
' Genius,' says Goethe, ' is that power in man which,

by living and acting, makes laws and rules.' But
the man who is such a genius that he *makes* laws
must of necessity *break* laws.   The *new* rule outrages
and violates the *old*.   The fashion of to-day is the
enemy of the mode of yesterday.   The genius
smashes his way through all the conventions.   There
will be frowns and scowls and pitiless criticism.
There will be crucifixion.   We have just celebrated
the centenary of Wagner.   Wagner was an original,
an eccentric, a genius—a poppy among the corn.
And, being a poppy, he carried a black cross in his
heart, and for years suffered the mortification of
seeing his best work driven from the stage by the
cat-calls and dog-whistles of his relentless critics.
The genius will come into his own at the last, but in
the meantime he must feel the sword piercing his
soul.

   Mr. F. W. H. Myers, in his critique upon Wordsworth, points out that Wordsworth represents
' what must always occur where an author, running
counter to the fashion of his age, has to create his
own public in defiance of the established critical
powers.   The disciples whom he draws round him
are for the most part young ;   the established
authorities are for the most part old ;   so that by the
time the original poet is about sixty years old,
most of his admirers are about forty and **most**

of his critics will be dead. His admirers now
become his accredited critics ; his works are widely
introduced to the public, and, if they are really
good, his reputation is secure.' The sun never
shines upon a finer spectacle than when it illumines
the fair young face of one who longs to teach the
old world some new lesson, to lift poor drab humanity
one inch nearer to the stars. It is very beautiful
for man or maid to aspire to being a poppy among
the corn. But beware ! Let no such aspirant forget
the black cross in the poppy's heart. When I think
of that, the poppies in the corn seem like splashes
of sacrificial blood upon the golden cornfield !

There is a very lovable thing about the poppies in
the corn that I can never sufficiently admire. The
poppies never belittle the corn. They glorify it.
You think not the less but the more of the corn
because of the presence of the poppies. At a rose
show one particularly radiant blossom puts to shame
all the surrounding roses. They are beggared by
comparison. That is because a show is all arti-
ficiality and affectation. Nature never humiliates
her more modest children in that ridiculous way.
As you watch the blood-red poppies tossing in a sea
of golden corn, it never occurs to you to institute
a comparison. The poppies and the corn seem
equally lovely. That is the glory of true greatness.

The Poppies in the Corn 279

Others are never humiliated in its presence. It elevates the mass. If the field were all poppies, its glory would have departed. The poppies need the corn. God makes nothing commonplace. Here is a gospel for those to whom the days seem grey because they have given up dreaming of being poppies :

A commonplace life, we say and we sigh,
 But why should we sigh as we say ?
The commonplace sun in the commonplace sky
 Makes up the commonplace day.
The moon and the stars are commonplace things,
And the flower that blooms and the bird that sings;
But dark were the world and sad our lot,
If the flowers failed and the sun shone not.
And God who studies each separate soul
Out of commonplace lives makes His beautiful whole.

God made the poppies, and He made the corn. He made the darkness, and He made the dawn. His morning and His evening made up one perfect day. His poppies and His corn are perfect parts of His perfect whole.

And if I rightly catch the meaning of their message, as the breeze whispers among the tall corn-stalks and flutters with the poppy's scarlet banners, they tell me that in this wondrous world work and rest are beautifully adjusted. I shall not labour the

point. Anybody can see that corn means toil.
Look at this ! It is a cornfield. I am quoting from
still another of Richard Jefferies' books. 'Never was
such work ! ' he says. ' The wages were low in those
days. The reaping was piece-work. So the reapers
worked and slaved and tore at the wheat as if they
were seized with a frenzy, the heat, the aches, the
illness, the sunstroke, always impending in the air.
It was nothing. No laugh, no song, no stay—on
from morning till night, possessed with a maddening
desire to labour. Their necks grew black, like
black oak in old houses. Their open chests were
always bare, and flat, and stark. The breastbone
was burned, and their arms, tough as ash, seemed
cased in leather. They grew visibly thinner in the
harvest fields, and shrunk together—all flesh dis-
appearing, and nothing but sinew and muscle
remaining. Never was such work ! ' I said that
anybody can see that corn means *toil*. And anybody
can see that the poppy means *rest*. The poppy is
the queen of opiates. Laudanum and opium are
her daughters. Myrtle Reed is the prophetess of
the poppy. Indeed, the smell of the poppy in her
stories is so strong as to be sometimes sickly. But
let me lay this pretty little sketch by Mr. Edgar Wade
Abbott beside Richard Jefferies' picture of the sweat
and strain of the cornfield :

The first train leaves at six p.m.
  For the land where the poppy blows;
The mother dear is the engineer,
  And the passenger laughs and crows.

The palace car is the mother's arms;
  The whistle, a low, sweet strain;
The passenger winks, and nods, and blinks,
  And goes to sleep in the train!

At eight p.m. the next train starts
  For the Poppy Land afar,
The summons clear falls on the ear;
  ' All aboard for the sleeping-car ! '

' But what is the fare to Poppy Land?
  I hope it is not too dear.'
The fare is this, a hug and a kiss,
  And it's paid to the engineer!

So I ask of Him who children took
  On His knee in kindness great;
' Take charge, I pray, of the trains each day;
  That leave at six and eight.

' Keep watch on the passengers,' thus I pray,
  ' For to me they are very dear;
And special ward, O gracious Lord,
  O'er the gentle engineer ! '

God never meant this field to be all corn, as it was
in Richard Jefferies' picture of the toilers among the
wheat ; nor all poppies, as in some of Myrtle Reed's

deathly scenes.   He sprinkles the poppies among the corn.   Labour and rest, as meted out by His hand, are very beautifully and very delicately adjusted.

But the poppies in the corn have kept their best secret till the last.   They tell me that they are simply a reflection of my own life and its deepest experiences.   And, now that I come to review that life of mine, it does look very much like a field of corn, with poppies here and there.   Most of our days are like the plain corn-stalks, but life is sprinkled with days that are conspicuous, scarlet, unforgettable.   ' There are days in spring,' says Richard Jefferies again, ' when the white clouds go swiftly past, with occasional breaks of bright sunshine lighting up a spot in the landscape.   That is like the memory of one's youth.   There is a long, dull blank, and then a brilliant streak of recollection.' Jefferies goes on to speak of the day when he fired his first gun and the day when he shot his first snipe. Michael Fairless, too, chats through a couple of pages about the great moments of her memory. There was the night when she was called up to see the moon's eclipse ; there was the night when she saw the huge seas breaking over the great lighthouse at Whitby ; there was the day when she found the first cowslips of spring, and sang to herself for pure joy of their colour and fragrance ; and there was the day when she first beheld the Rhine. We all find such poppies in our corn. There was Charles Lamb's great day when he visited the home of the Wordsworths, waded up the bed of Lodore, and clambered up to the top of Skiddaw. ' It was fairyland ! ' he says. ' That day will stand out like a mountain in my life ! ' What a day was that when George Borrow opened a copy of *Robinson Crusoe* ! or when Samuel Johnson found Law's *Serious Call* ! or when Robert Chambers discovered the *Encyclopaedia Britannica* ! ' My life,' says Chambers, ' was dark and cheerless till one day I found a copy of the *Encyclopaedia Britannica* in a cupboard in an attic. I learned from it that there were such things as literature, and astronomy, and geology. It was like cutting a window in a jail-cell through which I saw the world and the heavens beyond ! ' Here are poppies among the corn ! Yes, and there are days that, like the poppy, look like splashes of blood on the cornfield—days with a black cross in the very heart of them. I snip an inch or so from the police-court column of a newspaper by way of illustration. ' A poor, faded little woman was brought into court as witness in a disagreeable case, involving very serious issues. The entire case depended on the fact that a paper had been signed on a certain day, and this the forlorn

little woman was prepared to prove. " You saw the
paper signed? " asked the opposing counsel in cross-
examination. " Yes, sir." " You take your oath
that it was the thirtieth of August ? " " I know it
was, sir." The lawyer, who thought another date
could be proved, assumed an exasperating smile, and
repeated her words. " You know it was ! And
now, be so good as to tell us just how you know it."
The poor little creature looked from one countenance
to another with wide, sorrowful eyes, as if she
sought understanding and sympathy. Then her
gaze rested on the face of the kindly judge. " I
know," she said, as if speaking to him alone, " because
that was the day my baby died ! " Here was a blood-
red poppy to suddenly flash out in a very ordinary
cornfield ! Or look at this :

> The world remembers on that day,
>   A nation's splendid victory ;
> *The day I first beheld your face*
>   Is all it means to me !
>
> Another day ! How could I reck
>   War, famine, earthquake, aught beside ?
> My heart knows only one event——
>   It was *the day you died* !

Here are notable poppies sprinkling life's golden
cornfield !

I was passing, the other evening, a certain mission-hall in Melbourne. I peeped in. A great crowd of rough-looking men and women were singing, many of them with manifest emotion :

> O happy day that fixed my choice,
> On Thee, my Saviour and my God !
> Well may this glowing heart rejoice,
> And tell its raptures all abroad.
> Happy day ! happy day !
> When Jesus washed my sins away.

If only I could have got to the backs of the minds of all these singers and investigated the 'happy days' that were surging through their memories as they sang, what poppies I should have seen bespangling these commonplace cornfields ! Conversion was a soul-stirring and sensational experience to these people. That day stands out like a poppy with scarlet petals (and always the Cross as its centre-piece) in the thoughts of these happy singers. Yes, it is impossible to think of the red, red poppy without thinking of the black, black Cross. That is why the day of the Cross is the ruddiest and most radiant poppy in the whole field of human history. It is the blood-mark which shall glorify and sanctify every ear of common corn as long as the world shall stand.